"A profound permission slip I didn't even know I needed. Through warm and gracious prose, Anjuli gently guides us through the process of naming feelings, actually feeling those feelings, and bringing every feeling before the Lord. This book is a gift that multiplies—fueling the inner work so many of us need in order to flourish."

Ashlee Gadd
founder of Coffee + Crumbs and author of *Create Anyway: The Joy of Pursuing Creativity in the Margins of Motherhood*

"*Feel* is the companion guide you didn't know you needed. In these pages, our emotions are liberated to claim the space they deserve but are often denied. Anjuli empowers us to identify, express, and honor our feelings while pointing us to Christ."

Yvette Henry
speaker, writer, cohost of *How Married Are You?!* podcast

"*Feel* is a beautiful liturgy for our emotions, offering profound insights into how feelings illuminate a pathway to prayer and deeper intimacy with God. With grace and compassion, Anjuli Paschall gently leads us through our feelings, inviting us to befriend each one along the way."

Dr. Alison Cook
therapist, podcast host, and author of *I Shouldn't Feel This Way* and *Boundaries for Your Soul*

"In *Feel*, Anjuli Paschall invites us to experience the love of God, no matter what emotions we are wading through, hiding from, or trying to understand. Her words gently walk us through a journey of facing our feelings and finding God there through prayer and His words. *Feel* is a gift."

Greta Eskridge
author of *Adventuring Together* and host of *The Greta Eskridge Podcast*

"With powerful vulnerability, *Feel* provides gorgeous language for the deep work of offering our humanity to God. I'm profoundly grateful for the way Anjuli models the sacred dance of being fully human, even as we remember again and again—God is with us."

Aundi Kolber, MA, LPC
therapist and author of *Try Softer*™ and *Strong like Water*

"In this thoughtful, soulful collection, Anjuli helps us name, make space for, and move through our feelings. With care and compassion, this book invites us to offer every emotion to the One who made us and loves us into wholeness."

Kayla Craig
author of *Every Season Sacred: Reflections, Prayers, and Invitations to Nourish Your Soul and Nurture Your Family throughout the Year* and *To Light Their Way: A Collection of Prayers and Liturgies for Parents*; creator of Liturgies for Parents

feel

A Collection of Liturgies Offering Hope for Every Complicated Emotion

Anjuli Paschall

BETHANYHOUSE
a division of Baker Publishing Group
Minneapolis, Minnesota

Published by Bethany House Publishers
Minneapolis, Minnesota
BethanyHouse.com

Bethany House Publishers is a division of
Baker Publishing Group, Grand Rapids, Michigan

Printed in the United States of America

Library of Congress Cataloging-in-Publication Data

Names: Paschall, Anjuli, author.
Title: Feel : a collection of liturgies offering hope for every complicated emotion / Anjuli Paschall.
Description: Minneapolis, Minnesota : Bethany House Publishers, a division of Baker Publishing Group, [2024] | Includes bibliographical references and index.
Identifiers: LCCN 2023050993 | ISBN 9780764238536 (cloth) | ISBN 9781493445257 (ebook)
Subjects: LCSH: Liturgies. | Prayers. | Devotional exercises.
Classification: LCC BV198 .P37 2024 | DDC 264—dc23/eng/20240209
LC record available at https://lccn.loc.gov/2023050993

Cover Design: Dan Pitts
Cover Images: Emily Musgrove Art

The author is represented by Alive Literary Agency.

Baker Publishing Group publications use paper produced from sustainable forestry practices and postconsumer waste whenever possible.

24 25 26 27 28 29 30 7 6 5 4 3 2 1

For Sam
For every time I've felt something,
and you waited to see me—thank you.
Thank you for seeing me
as someone worth waiting for.

contents

a note to the reader

I'm not sure how this book found its way into your hands. Perhaps you've always been a nonfeeler and your feeler friend gave it to you as a gift. Maybe you are the one labeled "feeler" and are hoping to find some solace in the company of another feeler. Maybe you've always been the one who could think your way through hard stuff pretty well, but your emotions have always been a bit inconvenient. Your emotions scare you. Maybe you were always the "strong one" and feelings made you weak. You don't like feeling weak. But for whatever reason, you are here now. And I think it takes a bunch of courage to confront your feelings, whether you're a therapist, kindergarten teacher, or biochemist. Don't be fooled, left- or right-brained people don't get a hall pass on feeling their emotions. Humans have a hard time knowing what to do with their feelings, and it doesn't have anything to do with being good at numbers or liking poetry.

Maybe I am qualified to write this book because I have fallen into every "feeler" category. Deep feeler, nonfeeler, judgy feeler annoyed by the "criers," avoidant feeler, and scared feeler who was paranoid in third grade that I'd be seated by Mindy, the overfeeler, when it was seating chart day. (Don't worry, Mindy turned out to be one of my best friends, so there is hope for us all.)

Growing up, I learned that some feelings were acceptable—happiness, creativity, peace. While other emotions were bad, dangerous, and even seen as sinful—anger, confusion, fear. It has taken years to reintegrate the "bad" feelings and to reorder the "good" ones. I went on quite a journey to realize that feelings are neither right nor wrong, but a guide to wholeness and a pathway to prayer.

For most people, including me, feelings are messy. Feelings become one more thing to deal with. Painful feelings get in the way. We get anxious, stuck, overwhelmed, or ashamed of feeling what we feel. Because feelings can be complicated, we manage, negotiate, avoid, drown in, or dismiss them entirely. We have so many strategies to not feel what we feel. Yet, when we enter our feelings even with squinty eyes and hopefully a nice friend by our side (perhaps a paid counselor and always Jesus), we find the mysterious joy of being fully human. We no longer feel all chopped up inside, finding wholeness, integration, union, and, ultimately, peace (even when the most intrusive feelings poke at us at three a.m.).

How do you feel?

You must start here, like it or not. Discerning how you feel is like trying on shoes. Every person fits into feelings differently, just like shoes, which means you might have to try on several feelings to figure out which one it is that you actually feel. As your feet require different shoes for whatever kind of walk, hike, skip, or jump you do, so your heart experiences different feelings at different times. But after you try on a few for the right fit, you discover which one is right for you. When you name the feeling you actually feel, your soul will expand just as when you put on the right pair of shoes. You'll sink into it with ease. Think Cinderella and the glass slipper. When you identify the feeling you feel, something kind of magical happens (even if the circumstance or feeling is not ideal).

Feelings are layered. It's rare that you feel just one feeling at a time. And feelings are nuanced. There is a difference between worry and anxiety and nervousness, even though they feel rather similar. Sadness, sorrow, and longing may sing in the same minor key, but they aren't the same note. You can also feel annoyed, grateful, and ashamed—all at the same time. As you wade through your feelings, one will stand out just slightly more pronounced than the others. It will form to your foot in a way that makes you feel grounded and able to actually walk forward.

If you are more visual, you will find illustrations throughout this book that might help you identify how you feel.

This book isn't to be read front to back, but according to how you feel. You'll notice there are three movements to each feeling chapter you read: *The Language for Feeling*, *A Liturgy for Feeling*, and *A Living Word*.

First section—*The Language for Feeling*

In the first section, *The Language for Feeling*, I invite you to feel what you feel. You don't have to fight or flee from your feelings, but simply feel them (easier said than done, I know). Oftentimes we don't have words for our feelings, and we get stuck in a dark, painful place, banging our heads against a wall. Giving our feelings language is like turning on the lights. We realize the wall was actually a door, and words help us open it.

Every feeling has a story. It began somewhere. Maybe it was this morning when your alarm rudely interrupted your restful sleep. Maybe it was a shot of hormones that spiked because human bodies have an unruly mind of their own. A bad night's sleep or waves of estrogen certainly impact your emotions. These ought not be discredited as the cause for feeling how you feel.

But neither can you discredit the story that triggered your feelings. Once you are able to name how you feel (find the right shoe), try tracing the story of how this emotion came to be an active part of your current mood. You may be able to trace your feelings as far back as your childhood or as recently as ten minutes ago. Either way, tracing the story of your feeling is a big chunk of finding your way through it. In this section, *The Language for Feeling*, I trace my feelings. I try to find words for the mess inside of me. I pay attention to my body and where my feelings reside in me. This is my vulnerable attempt to share the words of my soul with you. Maybe in reading my words, you will find yours. Maybe retracing some of my stories will help you retrace yours.

This section is me trying to be a little more honest with you and my own heart. Welcome to my diary—unlocked and sold on Amazon for the same price as a bucket hat. God, help me.

We all have an inner outer space right below our rib cages. It gets scary in there. It can feel desolate, endless, and expansive. As I explore the cosmos within me, may you go on your own expedition. If my language for feelings helps you, wonderful. If not, skip right to the liturgies. There are no rules to this book. Pick your own adventure.

Second section—*A Liturgy for Feeling*

Open your heart and pray.

That sounds so simple, right? It isn't. We talk about prayer, we think about prayer, we tell people we will pray, but do we pray? We don't pray nearly as much as we talk about it or just think about our problems. (I'm speaking from my own personal experience.) This won't be a book that teaches you how to pray, but I hope it helps you actually pray.

Warning: Please don't expect this book to work like magic. You will be tempted toward "magical prayers." A magical prayer is the hope that Jesus would just fix how you feel, solve your problems, or take away your pain. But God's relationship with you is not transactional. You don't give Him your fear, and in exchange, He gives you instant peace. No, God is not a genie. Although God could miraculously heal you, God sometimes doesn't. Your relationship with God is just that—a relationship. Like a good parent, He wants you to find deep healing, not a temporary fix. This takes intentional time, contemplation, and a loving community that will bear witness to your wounds. God won't just put a bandage on your pain; He promises to come beside you in the process. God's unconditional aim is to carry you, comfort you, and offer you love as your story unfolds.

If you bought this book for a Hail-Mary, Lord-heal-me-now experience, return it. My goal is not to resolve your complicated feelings. For the record, even "happy" emotions can be complicated.

My hope is to invite you to feel what you feel as a way to connect with God. Feelings become a bridge to true connection. Yes, feelings create direct access to your creator. So in a way, feelings are a bit magical. The magic isn't in the resolution of your feelings, but the companionship God offers you all the way through them.

In this section, *A Liturgy for Feeling*, I hope you can pray. In honesty, cry out to God. In honesty, open your heart to God. Isn't this true prayer? Borrow my words if it helps. If words are too hard, sobs, silence, and soft sighs work too.

Last section—*A Living Word*

This section is an invitation to listen. For the talkers, those anxious about silence, and those who don't believe that God speaks, this might be a challenge. But God, like a good counselor, listens and speaks. His truth cuts to the core. It bypasses all your shenanigans and pierces your soul. After you've been honest with yourself and honest with God, listen. Listen to God's response to you. Listen to God's promises to you.

Every feeling can be found in Scripture. I marvel at this reality. Every single thing you feel isn't just mentioned in the Bible, but is actually experienced by people like Abraham, Moses, the minor characters like lowly shepherds and servants, Mary, and yes . . . Jesus. The book of Psalms is an entire book of the Bible filled with feelings in the form of prayers. Listen to the ways the Lord speaks into your emotions through Scripture. His living Word is filled with words of love. Listen.

A final note, friend.

I think it's important for you to know that I don't believe feelings tell you what to do. If you follow feelings alone, they will certainly lead you to folly. Just don't do it. I like to think of feelings like a map. When you feel lost, you roll out a map and you see three words in red letters: "You are here." Yup, this is the role of feelings.

They tell you where you really are. They aren't meant to tell you where to go or who you are. They serve you by helping you find your balance in the place where you actually are.

Feelings are an indicator that your soul needs more care. They are an invitation. If you follow the invitation, you will discover not just your own soul, but the presence of God with you. Your emotions became a doorway to prayer and—ultimately—love. Feelings become lights on the path, helping you see where your heart actually is.

It's possible that you can experience your feelings like a jewelry box and not like a junk drawer crammed with everything unwanted and displaced. It's possible for the nonfeelers and feelers to find freedom. It's possible that you don't have to be alone in figuring out the complicated places within you.

My hope is that this book will reside as a guide for you today and for years to come. Your feelings don't have to send you into a frenzy, a spiral, or a stress cycle. Feelings don't have to punish, paralyze, panic, pressure, or push you. The goal isn't to rid yourself of all feelings or just resolve the painful ones. Rather, my hope is that you experience the fullness of God's love in your life whatever emotions you're feeling, from exuberant joy to deep sorrow.

May this book be a gentle reminder that feelings are, more than anything, a gift.

Love always,
Anjuli

Start here: How do you feel?

How do you feel?

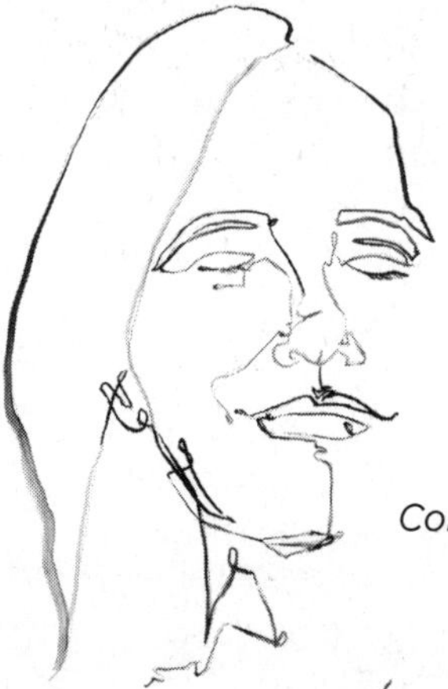

Content

Sad

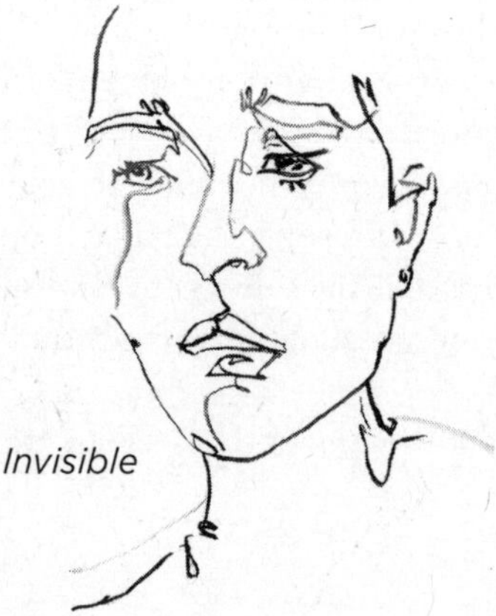

Invisible

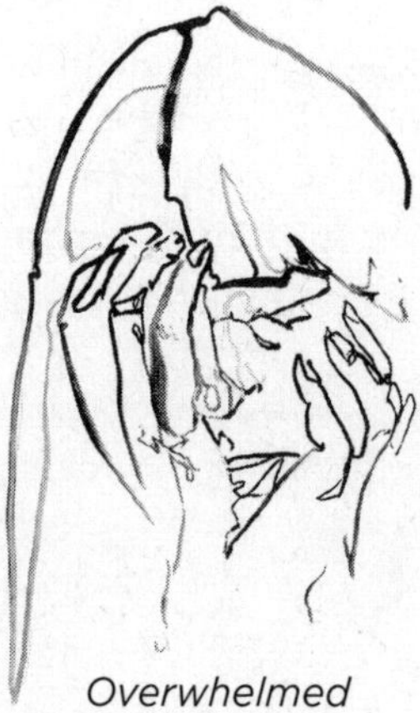

Overwhelmed

Discouraged

Resentful

Embarassed

Happy

Annoyed

Disgust

Anger

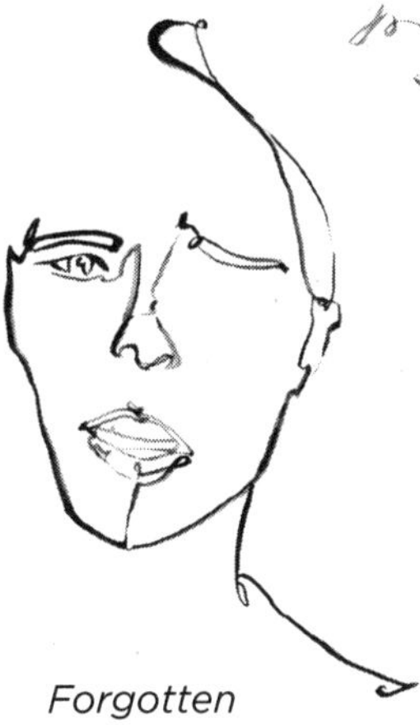

Forgotten

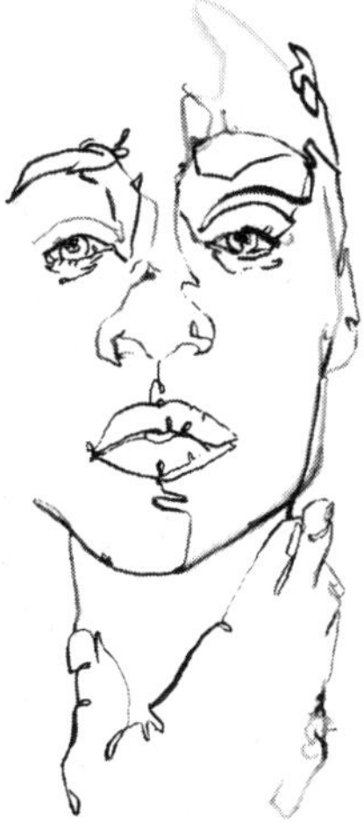

Helpless

How do you feel?

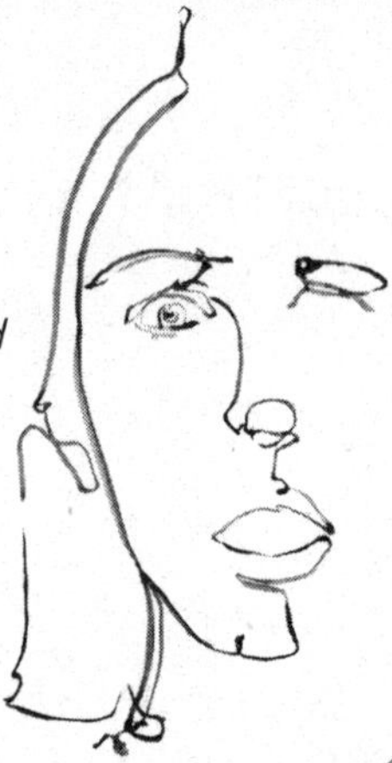

Shocked

Furious

Soft

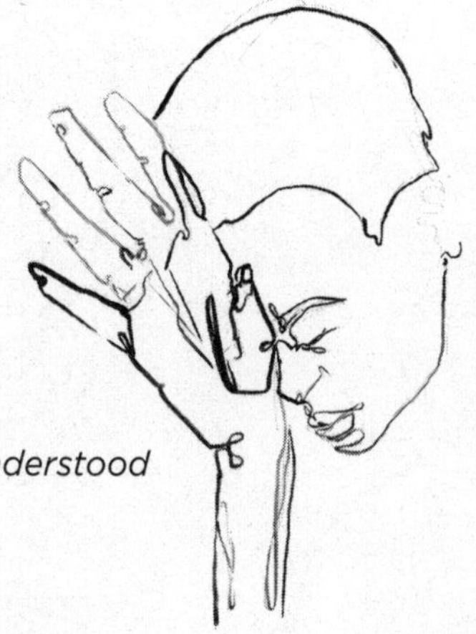

Misunderstood

Nostaligic

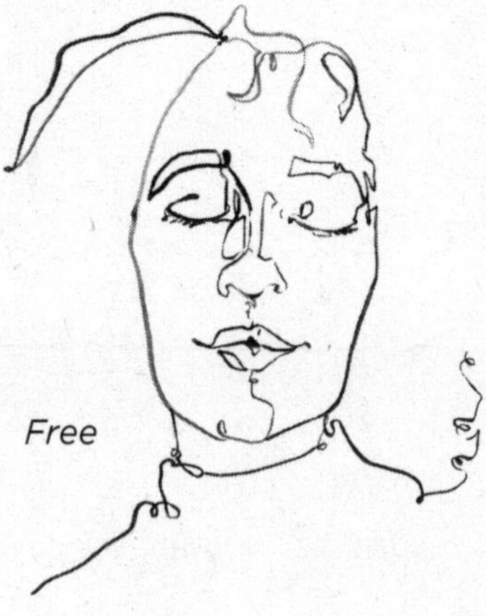

Free

Afraid

Awkward

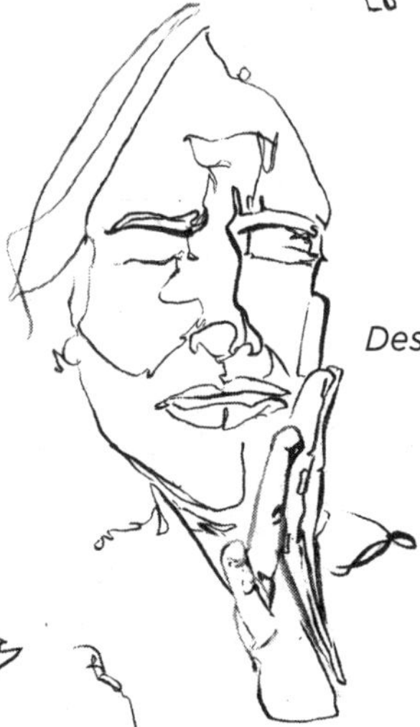

Desperate

Excited

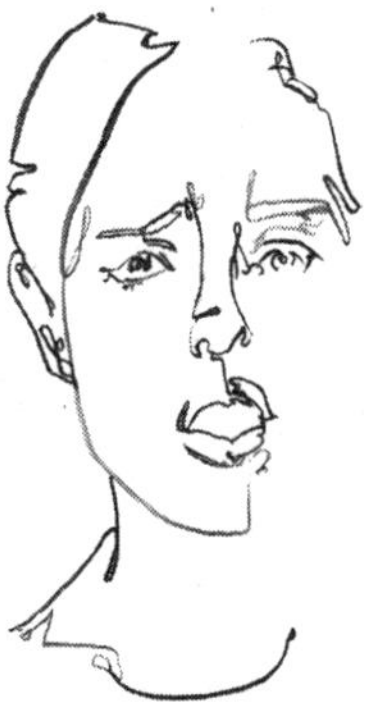

Betrayed

Surprise

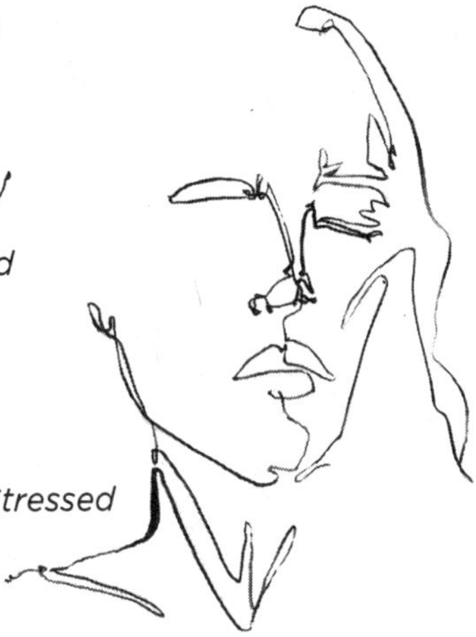

Stressed

1

surprise

Surprised—reaction to an unexpected or astonishing event, fact, or thing

Amazed—full of great wonder mixed with slight fear and awe

Excited—a heightened state of enthusiasm and eagerness

Disappointed—displeased because someone or something has failed to fulfill your hopes or expectations

Confused—unable to think clearly, uncertain

Awkward—feeling uneasy or uncomfortable

Disillusioned—disappointed that someone or something is less good than you had believed

Shocked—the result of a sudden upsetting or unsettling event or experience

surprised

reaction to an unexpected or astonishing event, fact, or thing

The Language for Feeling Surprised

Some people love surprises. They love pushing the boundaries of their bodies and emotions. They love the unknown. This is not the case for me. The thought of someone throwing me a surprise party makes me physically uneasy. I like life to be a tad bit more predictable. I like to know my surroundings and what I can expect. I like control. Surprises put me in a place of conflict. I feel split in two.

Today when a house full of unexpected guests came over for dinner, I was in conflict between my desire and my reality. I could see the potential for good. I could see the joy. But I was also aware of the struggle inside of me. Because I was caught off guard, I felt agitated. I wanted to blame someone for putting me in this position. This unexpected turn robbed me of control. I wanted to be more excited or happy or content, so I performed because I didn't know how to handle the situation. I pushed down my desires and gave people what they wanted even when I was not entirely happy. I gave people parts of me that I thought they could handle. But really, underneath it all, I felt missed. I felt pressure to please people who would be disappointed by my frustration. The easiest option was to hide myself away and just go through the motions.

My feelings sit in my chest, pulse through my arms, and beat in my heart. My senses are at attention, my muscles are on alert, adrenaline courses through me. I feel so many things at once. I trust God is here, but in the mix of all my complicated emotions, I wonder where He is.

A Liturgy for When I Feel Surprised

Breathe in—*God, help me . . .*
Breathe out—*trust in You.*

I open my heart.
God, I feel surprised.
I let myself feel this feeling.
My heart is fluttered.
I don't fully know why I feel the way I do, but here I am.
I am a mixture of many emotions.

You welcome me not as I should be, but as I am.
So I open my heart to You in truth.

As You have led me before, I trust You will lead me now.
Even when I don't know how to respond, what to say, or what to do next, I believe that you will give me what I need when I need it.
I am tempted to stand on my emotions that sway high to low, but instead, I stand on the trust that has been built between us all these years.

You see me.
You receive me.
You are with me.

Where I am right now isn't unknown to You.

You see all the sharp turns.
You have set every limit in place.
Nothing is beyond Your control.

I believe this surprise does not surprise You.
In ways I don't understand, You have even willed my circumstances for my good.

As I can, I receive this place I find myself in even though I feel fractured.
I trust that, in time, You will make all things clear.

I trust there is a gift in the making for me even though I don't fully understand it.

I give You thanks.
For it is in this place of surprise that Your grace meets me.

Living Word

I want to hear from You, God.

> ***John 13:6***
> He came to Simon Peter, who said to him, "Lord, do you wash my feet?"

amazed

full of great wonder mixed with slight fear and awe

The Language for Feeling Amazed

I stand at the edge of what feels like eternity. The sea and the sky are the same color steel. A mirror image of magic. I can barely see where the ocean ends and the atmosphere begins. In the stillness, I notice how at ease my soul feels. Wonder washes over me. I feel a faint tremble in my spirit. I am not afraid. I am aware of how small I am in this big world. A coolness washes over me. But I'm not cold, I am free.

I feel something more than awe. I feel amazed. A part of me wants to look away because this feeling overwhelms me. I never want it to end. I want more and more of it. Amazement is a powerful sensation. It feeds a deep hunger inside of me. I feel awake to the life I have always been craving. I savor this feeling. I experience something so profound that it stirs up inside of me a little fear. I feel this in my body. My eyes widen, my chest expands, and my breath slows.

I feel my soul tremble. I feel my delight grow. I feel my quiet nervousness. In my amazement, I sense the presence of God.

A Liturgy for When I Feel Amazed

Breathe in—*My Lord God*
Breathe out—*thank You.*

I open my heart to You.

I feel amazed.

My soul is expanding.

God, I ask for discernment.
Experiences that provoke the feeling of awe can also bind my soul in folly.
Evil can come disguised as an angel of light to dazzle.
Yet that dazzlement can be the instrument used to ensnare my soul.

Lord, may I be led by wisdom.

I have traveled quite a distance.
I have journeyed the long terrain of relationships or the rugged landscape of a mountainside.
I am surprised by the sheer beauty of what I behold.
My anticipation grows and delight dances within me.

God, what I've encountered is beyond what my soul was expecting.
Beauty pulls me right up next to my fragility; this frightens me.
Help me receive both fear and wonder as a gift.

My feelings of awe move me into an eternal space.
My soul touches something that transcends the borders that my body knows.

I am witnessing something holy.
God, I bear witness to Your beauty.
I refuse to seize control, run away, or grab on tighter.

Instead, I let myself enjoy what I see, sense, and feel.

Lord, I will not lose myself here, but instead, I discover new parts of me. I lift my eyes up. I lift my heart up. I lift my thoughts up to You, maker of heaven and earth. I look upon the masterpiece in front of me, inside of me.

You make beautiful things.

I marvel.

Lord, You've given me a glimpse at the hidden glory of heaven. The most elaborate display of Your glory is the company You have given me in Christ.

God, I know this moment will pass, and when it does I will let it. What I am experiencing now is just a foretaste of what is to come as time unfolds.

My heart is full of hope.

I feel Your love for me, and I bless Your name.

For this moment, my God, for what I witness now, I say, "Thank You, thank You, thank You."

Living Word

I incline my heart to listen to You.

> ***Luke 2:8–14***
> And in the same region there were shepherds out in the field, keeping watch over their flock by night. And an angel of the Lord appeared to them, and the glory of the Lord shone around them, and they were filled with great fear. And the angel said to them, "Fear not, for behold, I bring you good news of great joy that will be for all the people. For unto you is born this day in the city of David a Savior, who is Christ the Lord. And this will be a sign for you: you will find a baby wrapped in swaddling cloths

and lying in a manger." And suddenly there was with the angel a multitude of the heavenly host praising God and saying,

"Glory to God in the highest, and on earth peace among those with whom he is pleased!"

excited

a heightened state of enthusiasm and eagerness

The Language for Feeling Excited

I've wanted this for so long and worked so hard to get here. Today when my offer got accepted, I nearly fell over. It just might be happening. I feared it never would. But I stand at the edge of possibility, and I feel so excited.

Everything inside of me is accelerating. My soul is finally coming into contact with its greatest desire. I can't sleep, eat, or stop smiling. I am so consumed by excitement that I can lose sight of reality and the real people in front of me. My feelings can lead me to a place of only looking inward. I want to sustain this feeling for as long as possible. A part of me resists this feeling. I've known this feeling before, and things didn't turn out the way I had hoped. Excitement scares me. I simmer down my joy with reason.

The truth is, I feel excited. I feel surprised. My body is fully awake. My heart is moving at a rapid pace. My thoughts dance. I can't sit still. I am overcome with enthusiasm for what is happening and what is to come.

Although this feeling of excitement can stir up anxiety and stress, I don't attend to those feelings. Instead, I turn my attention to God with my excitement.

A Liturgy for When I Feel Excited

Breathe in—*God, my Father . . .*
Breathe out—*You are good.*

I open my heart to You, God.

I feel excited.

I am surprised by how I feel.

Excitement has played a part in my story. In ways, my excitement may not have been nurtured or known. In ways, my excitement may feel uncomfortable.

I pause to let You attend to my heart now.

You, God, are writing anew in my life, and I eagerly and anxiously await what You will do.

God, I want to be mindful of the source of my excitement.
Is the thing that is exciting me truly from You, or am I attaching Your name to it as a free pass to do what I want?

Search my heart, O God.

My life stands on the edge of something new. The goodness of what I am receiving catches me off guard.

My life is a miracle. I am experiencing the fullness of what that means right now. My circumstances, the people, and the possibilities before me are all unexpected gifts. Excitement is my response to these gifts. Even though I am tempted to control the gifts, I resist. Even though my soul can creep toward fear, I resist. For a moment, I receive this excitement as a gift right now.

I clap along with nature. I sing in harmony with the sounds of salvation. I explore the possibilities. I let excitement ignite my senses. I stand amazed at the site I gaze upon. I look upon the goodness now and to come, but what I marvel at is that You know me and love me in a way that no one else can. You are penning a story that leaves me in awe and anticipation.

I present my life to You with all that is unknown and all that is yet to come.

I delight in You.
Thank You, God, for this joy.

My excitement will come and go.
The tune of my life circumstances will change, but God, You never will.
I feel my excitement. I savor and soak it up.
I give thanks for what has come to pass, for today, and what will come tomorrow.

Even here, my heart clings to You.
Even here, my eyes look up to the heavens.
Even here, my soul finds its greatest satisfaction in You.

You love to give me good gifts.

For this, I give thanks.

Living Word

I will listen to You.

Psalm 37:3–6

Trust in the LORD, and do good;
    dwell in the land and befriend faithfulness.
Delight yourself in the LORD,
    and he will give you the desires of your heart.
Commit your way to the LORD;
    trust in him, and he will act.
He will bring forth your righteousness as the light,
    and your justice as the noonday.

disappointed

displeased because someone or something has failed to fulfill your hopes or expectations

The Language for Feeling Disappointed

I wanted the position. It seemed so perfect. I had the right connections. I had the right qualifications. But in the end, it didn't work out, and I'm left wondering why and what's wrong with me. I'm left feeling a bit stunned.

I tried so hard. I can't explain it. It doesn't make sense. This door closing feels like a hammer to my heart. I feel shut down and even bothered. I feel embarrassed that I was ever excited about this possibility in the first place. I want to make sense of it, but I can't. I strategize a new plan. I push through my disappointment by distracting myself. But subtly, self-pity, accusations, and wallowing sneak in. Passive aggressively, I attempt to acquire sympathy from others. I pull away and parts of me are pushed down. I wish I had never tried at all.

The truth is I feel disappointed, which leads to confusion. I feel hurt, upset, let down. I feel weary. These feelings stick to me. I feel disappointment in my body. I feel heavy, my neck hurts, my back tightens, my chest aches. I am stunned.

I don't want to open my heart up at all. If I am honest, it stings more than I want to admit. Hope deferred makes my soul sick. I stay here. I feel what I feel without negotiating with myself or ignoring my true emotions. I want things to be different. I am tired. But what I want more than life on my terms is to know that God hasn't forgotten about me.

A Liturgy for When I Feel Disappointed

Breathe in—*Jesus, . . .*
Breathe out—*You restore my hope.*

God, I open my heart to You.

I feel disappointed.

For a moment, I allow myself to feel what I feel.

Search my heart, O God.
When in my story have I felt this feeling before?

My feelings of disappointment are a signal to me that my soul needs Your care.

I want to see myself honestly.
Were my expectations misplaced, misguided, or unrealistic?
Were my hopes properly ordered under You, God?

My desires weren't met.
I am surprised by how things turned out.

I deeply hoped something or someone would have provided a way for me to be free, find connection, feel valued, or experience love.
Instead, I feel shocked, hurt, sad, upset, and unseen.

As it remains, I am powerless to change my situation, but rather I must accept it.

I surrender my imagination to You.
I release a future I cannot control.
I open my heart to receive the life You have given me today even with its challenges.

I pour out my sorrow to You.
It is a sorrow I have felt before.
Even though I feel disoriented, I will trust You.
You will meet me in my ache with kindness.
You will care for my life and quiet longings.

You will.
I trust that You will tend to my desires.
I doubt Your good will for me at times, but help me stand more secure in Your love for me than anything else.

Every moment and every morning You meet me.
Even when I only set my gaze on getting something, being with someone, or going somewhere, You gently nudge me to look at You.

You heal my soul with new mercies.
God, You give me a new day.
You grant me a new perspective.
You remind me to slow down and see Your gifts.
You hear me now.

O Lord, plant seeds of new hope inside my soul.

Where people fail, where plans fail; where dreams fail, where I fail myself—Your mercies never fail.

Yes, I feel so many mixed emotions.
Yes, life and people aren't as I imagined they would be.
Yes, I feel disappointed.
I will remain and return here—to Your expansive love.
Your love comes again and again like the morning sun.

Restore my hope, O God.
I set my hope on You alone.
My lips will continue to praise You.

Even here, I give You thanks because through my feelings of disappointment, You meet me.

Living Word

I turn my heart to Your words of life.

> ***Lamentations 3:22–23*** *NIV*
> Because of the LORD's great love we are not consumed,
> for his compassions never fail.
> They are new every morning;
> great is your faithfulness.

confused

unable to think clearly, uncertain

The Language for Feeling Confused

If I end the relationship, I am afraid it will end me. But if I stay in it, I might forever feel sad. What's worse? The fear of hurting someone, or bearing the weight of pain indefinitely? My worry consumes me. I can't think straight. A dense fog clouds my ability to see. Any step forward seems like it will lead me down an impossible path. I feel uncertain. I can't see a future that doesn't involve some sort of discomfort. Postponing a decision feels like the safest thing to do, but it also makes me feel more anxious. I want to regain control. I feel the weight of responsibility on me. A part of me wants to just run away and escape everything. I don't want this challenge before me. I want to hide. I am looking for distractions all the time.

I'm not indecisive. Indecisiveness is having clarity of the choices before me but lacking the ability to pick a path. I feel confused. I don't have the ability to see my choices because fear clouds everything I see. I am bound up by many things. I am conflicted.

For a moment, I let myself feel what I feel without moving to action or trying to figure everything out. I feel the heaviness of my confusion in my body. I feel disconnected, distracted, and even disoriented. Something is gnawing away at me. My gut is churning. My chest feels heavy. The eyes of my heart and mind are darting from one place to the next. My thoughts bend and twist.

I want a lot of things, but more than anything, I want to do what is right in the eyes of God. Slowness, prayer, and patience are hard for me, but I know this is the way of wisdom. As I listen to what I really want, I want what God wants for me.

A Liturgy for When I Feel Confused

Breathe in—*Jesus, help me . . .*
Breathe out—*wait with You.*

God, I open my heart to You.

I feel confused.

For a moment, I let myself feel what I feel.

I feel it in my body.

I want to be attentive to when I've experienced this feeling in my story before.

The way forward is unclear.
I am afraid because it seems like every option before me is hard.
I am afraid.

Help me see what I am really afraid of.

I am in distress.
My desires conflict with one another.

I am fatigued by trying to figure everything out.
I am weary from working so hard to find a way.
My mind is exhausted from thinking, and my body is beat down.
I tend to doubt myself.
I tend to doubt You.

But You invite me to slow down.
You invite me even when I am scattered and dizzy.

I stop and wait here.
I pull over and regain composure on the soul side of the street.
I don't have to figure anything out at this moment.
I don't have to decide anything at this time.
I can be here and let You love me in this unresolved place.

What I need more than anything is Your assurance that I am not alone in this.

God, in all the unknown, I am reminded of what I do know.
You are sovereign.
You know me.
You have faithfully walked in pace with me up to this point.
You will never leave me.
You have always made a way.

I wait, trust, and remember that You are near.

In my feelings of great confusion, I release my life into Your care.
For You are good to those who trust in You.

Help me have the courage to look where I don't want to look.
Help me lean on those whom I trust for wisdom.
Help me listen to my voice and my deepest desires.

Gift me with words that are true and keep me sturdy.
Gift me with the capacity to be kind to myself in all that remains unknown.
Gift me with discernment to know Your will, and give me ears to hear the deepest peace within me.

Help me hear the voice of truth, that I may rest.

When some voices draw me into deeper confusion, may I remain strong in what I know to be right, good, and in line with who You are and who You have created me to be.

Illuminate the path You would have me walk down by guiding my heart in even the faintest peace and truth that reside inside of me.

Even here, fear may still plague me, but I trust that Your love will pave the way that leads me closer to You.

Even here, I give thanks for my feelings of confusion because they have led me here to You.

Even here, I will bless Your name.

Living Word

I will listen to You.

> ***Psalm 119:34–37*** *NASB*
> Give me understanding, that I may observe Your law
> And keep it with all my heart.
> Make me walk in the path of Your commandments,
> For I delight in it.
> Incline my heart to Your testimonies
> And not to dishonest gain.
> Turn away my eyes from looking at vanity,
> And revive me in Your ways.

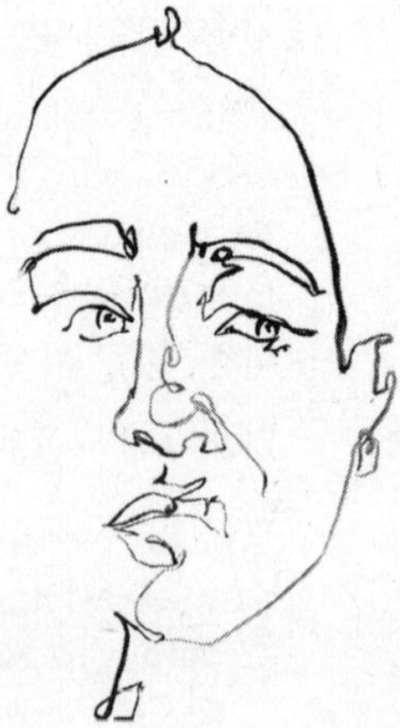

awkward

feeling uneasy or uncomfortable

The Language for Feeling Awkward

I remember the night of the wedding. I wore a gold satin dress because I was a bridesmaid. I was in the inner circle but felt on the outside. During the reception, with my back against the bathroom stall I cried. Dark mascara spots splattered down my pretty dress and I felt all alone. Black tears don't wash out of gold satin no matter how hard you scrub.

I've locked myself away behind invisible doors that often promise protection. Doors like bathroom stalls, bedrooms, and my own skin, I've tried to escape. I've had a hard time fitting in. Coming out from behind these straw walls feels dreadfully uncomfortable. I'd rather hide myself away than face the reality of my own awkward feelings. I want to control my feelings. I can even weaponize shame to make others feel bad for making me feel uncomfortable. It's embarrassing, but true. I am tempted to withdraw. I avoid the person, place, or thing that triggers my unease. Something must be wrong with me.

Somehow, I've managed. I get through the social interaction. I get through the uncomfortable thing. But I'm always on edge because I never know when I'll feel awkward. Sometimes it comes out of nowhere and surprises me. I feel awkward right now. I feel it in my body. My chest feels tense, and my gut is swirling. My thoughts are scattered. I feel uncomfortable in my own skin.

Something is being asked of me. I feel awkward because I am in a situation where I can't show up fully as myself. I feel like I have to change or conform to an environment to be safe or liked. I can't show up as I am. I don't know how to be myself. The more I try to hide my awkwardness, the more I believe people see it. I don't want to feel this way anymore. I want a way through this where I am not bound up by the pressure to be something or someone else.

A Liturgy for When I Feel Awkward

Breathe in—*O Lord . . .*
Breathe out—*I present myself to You.*

I feel awkward right now.

This is an uncomfortable feeling, but I allow myself to feel what I feel.

I have felt like I don't belong before.

I present myself to You, Lord.
My awkwardness is not a disruption or distraction to You, God.
You welcome all of me.
You don't ask me to alter myself before I come to You. Rather, You insist that I come as I am.

In You, Jesus, I belong.

Help me turn my sight from seeing only my shortcomings to seeing the welcoming grace You offer me, God.

Your grace welcomes me again and again and again.
Yes, all of me.
Me, with my differentness.
Me, with nothing to offer.
Me, with my conflict.
Me, who feels weird.
Me, who has been hurt or has caused hurt.

Grace makes room for me to belong in the middle of my messy feelings. Not just a part of me.
Not just a piece of me.
But all of me is welcome to come in, be seen, and take up space.

I was never meant to live a life of running, hiding, or pretending.
It is through my weaknesses that I discover more and more grace.
My awkwardness is not a prison I must escape, but a place I allow Your grace to enter in.
I was called to a life of grace.

My awkwardness becomes my guide to grace.
Grace leads me back to the endless welcome of Christ.
With You, God, my identity is rooted.
With You, God, I am fully known.
With You, God, I am formed in love.

I bring the fumbling, bumbling, awkward mess of who I am to You.
With You there is warm welcome.

Living Word

I want to hear what You say to me.

> ***Exodus 4:10–13***
> But Moses said to the LORD, "Oh, my Lord, I am not eloquent, either in the past or since you have spoken to your servant, but I am slow of speech and of tongue." Then the LORD said to him, "Who has made man's mouth? Who makes him mute, or deaf, or seeing, or blind? Is it not I, the LORD? Now therefore go, and I will be with your mouth and teach you what you shall speak." But he said, "Oh, my Lord, please send someone else."

disillusioned

disappointed that someone or something is less good than you had believed

The Language for Feeling Disillusioned

I thought I knew you. I thought we lived with an unspoken vow of honesty. I believed that you were one of the safe ones. But I guess I didn't see you as clearly as I thought I did. I trusted the person you said you were. I was wrong. I'm left wondering what was even real. I feel tricked, betrayed.

I want to make sense of what happened, because it doesn't make sense. I think, process, and try to fix the person or situation as though it were a problem with a solution. Reason seems like my greatest resource to get through this. I also want to cling to the illusion because I so badly wish it were true. I wish you were who you said you were. I don't want to feel this way. I press forward without processing the loss because it seems like the easiest solution. But how could I have let this happen? What's wrong with me? How could I have been so foolish? I believed so blindly.

I feel disillusioned. I can't wrap my mind around what has happened. How can it be that I didn't see the signs? How is it possible that the person in my life that I trusted wasn't who I thought he was? I feel stunned. I feel confused. I feel hurt. I can't make sense of this. I know this is not a mystery I am meant to solve, but a story I am meant to enter. Where do I go from here?

A Liturgy for When I Feel Disillusioned

Breathe in—*My Lord God . . .*
Breathe out—*help reorient me to what is real.*

I open my heart to You.

I feel disillusioned.

For a moment, I allow myself to feel what I feel.

I let my body feel this ache.

When in my life have I felt this way before, God?
I was deceived.
I believed something was good when, in fact, it was not.
Such a deception is jarring, painful, and confusing.
I am left in a daze, asking, "What was real?"

Confusing feelings swirl within me—anger, sadness, longing, resentment, and fear.
My heart was invested.

God, I don't want to become cynical, judgmental, closed off, and condescending.
I don't want to feel like this forever.
I don't know what to do.

God, for reasons I don't fully understand, this relationship or circumstance has been removed from my life.
I am powerless to change others, but I can control how I respond.

Now I am entering a new reality.
The reality is that You remain true.

God, help reorient me to what is real now that my world has changed.
Help me see what is true about You, me, and others in the midst of all that is false.
Help me think clearly about everything that is unclear.
Help me understand what is necessary for me to understand.

God, I redirect my eyes back to You.
May my soul regain the love it has lost.
I trust You with my anger.
I trust You with my sadness.
I trust You with my pain.
I trust You with all that remains unknown.
I trust that, in Your will and in Your way, You will restore my soul.

Even here, You are writing a new story.

Lord, hear my prayer.

Living Word

You speak words of life and I will listen.

> ***Ephesians 4:32***
> Be kind to one another, tenderhearted, forgiving one another, as God in Christ forgave you.

shocked

the result of a sudden upsetting or unsettling event or experience

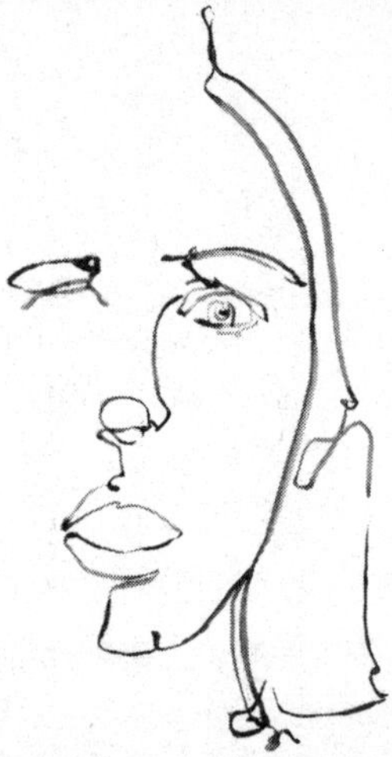

The Language for Feeling Shocked

One second she was here and the next second she was gone. How, with the ring of one phone call, could my life radically change? I feel like someone slapped my face with a frozen glove. I'm stunned.

Waves of disbelief and confusion pulse through me. I almost feel numb, yet there is a storm inside of me.

I feel shocked. I don't want to face this scary thing. It feels so confusing. I just want to regain control over my emotions. I try to control others or details or time or food. I just want something that can stabilize me. My body feels stunned. I almost feel like I'm outside of it. I try to let all of my shock settle in. Something substantial has happened. I was caught off guard. The earth in which I walked has been shaken. Nothing I do can change that. No action now can alter what has already been done. I let the aftershocks shake through me.

I don't want to deal with my feelings. It feels like too much. I am scared of what damage is deep down there. I just want to move on. I want out. I can't handle anything else. But the truth is, I do not want to become more broken by the event that has shocked me. I don't want it to permanently hurt me. I want to become more whole because of it. I want to find a wise way through this.

A Liturgy for When I Feel Shocked

Breathe in—*Lord, beneath the storm . . .*
Breathe out—*You are my stillness.*

I turn to You now, God.

I feel shocked.

In the abruptness of everything, I allow myself to feel what I feel.

I pay attention to when in my story I have felt this way before.

Lord, I listen for Your voice.
This is hard for me because I want to find answers and reasons. I want to calculate who is at fault.

I want to replay the situation and imagine a different outcome.
I may be tempted to hurry my way through this.
I may be tempted to doubt Your goodness.
I may be tempted to avoid pain from my past, present, and future.

I hold my feelings in my body.
I touch my chest, my throat, my head.
I slow down.

God, help me.
The only way forward is with Your help.
As I wait for my shock to settle, I listen to Your voice.
I listen to You in the stillness.

Your healing voice is found in the quiet whispers of peace dripping like an IV into my soul.
You cocoon my spirit and absorb the shock waves.
You bind my wounds.
Even as shocking as the situation may be, You remain absolutely unchanged and unshocked.
You care for my good and the good of those I love.
I try to believe this even if it is hard.
Even if no sense can be made of the nonsense in my life,
I will stand firm in You.

I listen to Your promises and my shock is sustained.
You are my shelter in my sadness.
You are my refuge for my anger.

You are my shield of protection against my enemies.
You are my hiding place when all I want to do is hide.

You guide me back to safe harbors.

Hour by hour, breath by breath, You attend to my life and those in my care.
I will not hurry, avoid, condemn, or neglect my soul.
I will trust that You will reconnect all that feels disconnected in me in time.
I listen to Your voice in the storm.

I open my heart to You.

Living Word

I want to hear what You have to say.

> ***1 Kings 19:12***
> And after the earthquake a fire, but the LORD was not in the fire. And after the fire the sound of a low whisper.

2

fear

Afraid—fearing that a bad thing will happen

Unworthy—feeling as though you have limited value

Helpless—feeling that there's no way out

Insecure—not being confident or assured, uncertain

Anxious—the general feeling of avoiding other important emotions

Stressed—having too much to do

Vulnerable—being exposed

Nervous—fearing that a good thing won't happen

Overwhelmed—being buried under the weight of too many things

Scared—fear that comes when something bad has happened or is happening

Desperate—feeling that nothing you can do is enough

Worried—concerned over a specific area of your life (money, health, work, relationships, time)

Guilty—fearing that punishment awaits you for a crime or wrongdoing you have committed

afraid

fearing that a bad thing will happen

The Language for Feeling Afraid

Our home was filled with beautiful chaos. People gathered, laughed, dined, and drank. After everyone said good-bye, I was left with a growing fear of all the bad things that could happen—injury, accident, death. The fear of what could happen to those I love constantly hovers over me. The scenarios always end in death. I panic, pace, and try to be proactive. Fear drives me. It echoes in the quiet spaces. It screams even in the safe places. I feel I must protect myself and those I love. It's an exhausting way to live, and tonight I am tired, but I can't calm the noise. I can't sleep.

I sometimes treat my fear as my enemy and fight it off. I can also believe that fear is my friend helping me predict the future. Fear consumes me. It whispers that I alone am responsible for the outcome of my life.

I don't like being afraid. I have to get rid of this feeling. I have to control it. I get defensive and on edge. My fear can be so overwhelming that I want to avoid it, distract it, and even use false optimism to overcome it. I feel small and weightless. Everything is a threat.

For a moment, I let my fear stay as neither friend nor foe, but simply for what it is—a feeling. I let it fill my chest and fill my lungs. My shoulders tighten. I let what is already within me be fully here. I pay attention to the movements of my soul and the way I try to resolve my feelings entirely alone.

My fear is deep. The depth of it is still unknown to me. That scares me. I am afraid to live without fear, but I don't know how to live with it. My heart is disordered. I don't want just a quick fix; I want heart healing. I want fear to hold the right place in my life.

A Liturgy for When I Feel Afraid

Breathe in—*My Lord God, help me . . .*
Breathe out—*rest in You.*

God, here I am.

I feel afraid.

I pay attention to where fear lives in my body.

Allow me to remember when I have felt fear in my story before.

God, I tend to reach for safety in my strength, strategies, and schedule.
I tend to reach for protection in my own power, prestige, and plan.
I tend to reach for refuge in my resources, research, and rightness.

Instead, I want to rest in You, God, my Father.
You are a soft place for me to land in my spiraling.
You reorient me to the reality of Your goodness.
You rescue me when all my efforts fall short.
You reconcile my heart to You, those I love, and even my enemies.

Please reorder all that is disordered within me.
Please realign fear to its rightful place.
Please remind me that darkness is not evil, but an opportunity for intimacy.

In my fear, You invite me to pray honestly.
In my fear, You call me to be close to You.
In my fear, You pull out a chair for me to be loved.

Search my heart.

What do You want me to know about You, God?

I trust You right now with my life.
I trust that what You say is true.
I trust Your words "Take heart, do not be afraid."

In the storm, even Peter faltered.
Peter, the *rock of the church*, sank like a pebble into the sea.
You don't demand perfection.
You invite me to seek Your eyes when everything around me is scary.

With all that is unknown today and tomorrow, I seek Your face.
I will entrust my life into Your care.

Whatever comes to pass, whatever I can't control, whatever You allow to happen—I will trust in the great mystery of Your sovereignty and providence.

I open my desires to You, God.
In the same breath, I release them.
As the waves lap on the shore, I learn that You give and take away.
Even when the circumstances are not as I wish, I will bless Your name.

I come into Your rest.
You rested in the storm.
You rested knowing that death was not the worst-case scenario.
You rested in Your Father's love.

I open my heart to You, knowing that as I experience my fear, I also get to experience Your love for me. Fear becomes a pathway for me to come into Your care.

For this, I give You thanks.

Living Word

I want to hear from You.

> ***Matthew 14:27***
> But immediately Jesus spoke to them, saying, "Take heart; it is I. Do not be afraid."

unworthy

feeling as though you have limited value

The Language for Feeling Unworthy

I scan the room. Everyone seems to have a place here but me. I pull out all my tricks. I work the room. I put on my best self. Humor, telling stories, showing interest in everyone are the ways I try to gain the affection of others. I search the room for eyes that are searching for mine. I am really looking for someone to approve of me. I try hard to say all the right things so I won't be outed as an impostor. I keep up the show and avoid revealing any weaknesses. But inside, I am so tired of keeping up the performance. I'm so tired of doing.

Doing is everything. Working on the outside makes me feel worthy on the inside. If I could just keep the peace, keep up with the performance, keep up the face, keep up the place, then everything would be okay. Then *I* would be okay. I search for others' affirming eyes to appease my own anxious spirit. I measure my worth by how others measure me. I am always grabbing, grappling, and grasping for affirmation.

I try to manage my feelings. I have a tendency to assume responsibility for things that are not my responsibility. If there is relational distance, it's my fault. If someone is disappointed, it's my fault. If someone is angry, it is my fault. My efforts to prove that I am worth keeping around leave me exhausted. My own needs are easily dismissed if it means getting or keeping love close.

I let these feelings of worthlessness stay for a moment. I make space for them even though I would rather not. I even pay attention to the stories this feeling is connected to. I take note of the memories that come to mind. For so long I believed my actions were the only way to get the love I desired.

My search for worth has only led me down a road of more and more fear. Yet even here, I want to believe that my worth is found in God. Like the Prodigal Son, I want to know You as the Father who awaits my arrival.

A Liturgy for When I Feel Unworthy

Breathe in—*Father, help me see how . . .*
Breathe out—*You come to me.*

I present my heart to You.

I feel unworthy.

This feeling is familiar to me. Veins of unworthiness are written throughout the story of my life.

I feel this feeling in my body.

O God, my heart feels weak, tired, and weary.
I worry about being "too much."
I fear being a burden or being too needy or not enough.

God, I open myself to You.
I bring every part of me that I've cut off or condemned—forward.
I bring my needs, desires, and dreams into the daylight too.

I bring me.

In response, You run toward me as You did the Prodigal Son.

Before I can speak a word, You run to me.
Before I can present my case, You pursue me.
Before I can clean up, there You are, coming after me.

You don't come because of my actions, words, goodness, gifts, confession, or offerings, but because I am Your joy.
Your delight in me is not dependent on me at all.

Help me be fully honest with myself and with You.

Even here, there is a part of me that doesn't want unconditional love.
I want to earn it, achieve it, deserve it, and get credit for it.
But I also want relief from the unending burden of proving myself.
I've tried so long and so hard to earn my seat at the table.

But Your table welcomes the bent out of shape, bland, boring, socially awkward, and stubborn.
Your table welcomes the late, lazy, overweight, captivating, and unimpressive.
Your table welcomes the tired, timid, and tripped up.
Your table welcomes uneducated, unorganized, and empty-handed people all the same.
You set the table with the finest foods and fancy silver.

I bring my sin and shortcomings to You.

You open the door.
You pull out a seat at the table for me to sit down.
I come.

When I search for the eyes that are searching for me, may it be Your eyes I see.

Your assurance is what sets my soul at ease.
When I receive your love, acceptance, and peace, I don't have to search anywhere else to find it.

God, I come to You.
You don't need me to take care of You.
You don't need me to prove myself.
You don't need me to be better.

You peer out the window.
You eagerly await my arrival.
You invite my tired heart to sit down and be seen.

Here, my worth is found, complete, and final.

Here, You reveal myself to me so I can see that I am seen.
As I feel my unworthiness, I am led to You. Even though feeling what I feel is hard, I believe it has led me back to You.

For this, I give You thanks.

Living Word

I will listen and believe that You love me.

> ***Luke 15:17–20***
> But when he came to himself, he said, "How many of my father's hired servants have more than enough bread, but I perish here with hunger! I will arise and go to my father, and I will say to him, 'Father, I have sinned against heaven and before you. I am no longer worthy to be called your son. Treat me as one of your hired servants.'" And he arose and came to his father. But while he was still a long way off, his father saw him and felt compassion, and ran and embraced him and kissed him.

helpless

feeling that there's no way out

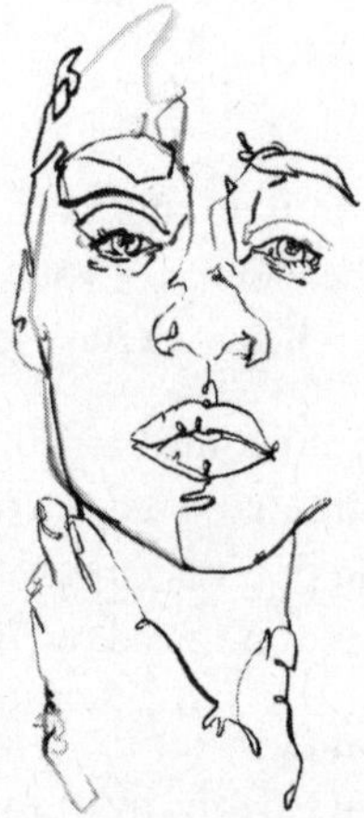

The Language for Feeling Helpless

I am alone. With my windows down, I listen to the waves pound the earth. One after the next they come. The sound of the water hurling over itself on the ocean floor echoes the feeling of my chest collapsing in on me. I tip my head back. Tears fall effortlessly with the rhythm of the waves. I want to crawl out to the sea and let the water sweep me away. But moving my body feels like more work than I can bear. So I stay in the dark because here, darkness is my companion. The sound of everything crashing is the only thing that can comfort my soul.

I feel helpless.

I want to climb out of the pit I find myself in. I dig my fingers into the mud, grabbing on to the stones, trying to claw my way out. On my back I carry all that is unsolvable, unfixable, unbearable. I want to stop entirely. I just can't do all this anymore. I can't grapple against earth and pain and people and fear any longer. So I lie down in the darkness. I believe tears are my only end. I have not only lost the battle; I have lost myself.

I am still here, but life is closing in on me with no apparent way out. Blackness is all around. I feel afraid. And now, I am tired. Very, very tired. I have come to the end of myself, and there is almost relief. Is it possible that God could meet me here?

A Liturgy for When I Feel Helpless

Breathe in—*Lord God . . .*
Breathe out—*You are with me here.*

I open my heart to You.

I feel helpless.

I feel helpless to help myself or others.

I feel it in my body.

Search my heart, O God.

Reveal to me when I have felt this feeling before, if ever.

God, it may be a faint whisper, an exhale, or a cry, but I release.
I let go.
I accept that I am helpless right now.
I am tired of trying.
I am exhausted from exerting so much effort.
I don't know what to do anymore.

I may be tempted to get lost in my sorrow.
I may be tempted to find comfort in anger, fear, or accusations.
I may be tempted to turn to myself for answers.

I am afraid for those I love.
I am afraid for myself.

I am afraid of what could happen or what has.

Am I beyond help?

You remain with me in the darkness.
You remain with me in my despair.
You remain with me in my desolation.
You remain with me in the unknown.

Let my silence, my slightest sigh or groan from the core of my existence be my prayer.
I let all of me curl up beside all of You.
In this darkness, I breathe.
In the unknown, I breathe.
I still have air in my lungs.

Faint and quiet is my breath, but it is here.
God, can my breath be enough?

God, You are with those I love.

God, You are with me here.
God, You are with me here.
God, You are with me here.

I wait for help to come.

I wait for You to part the sea.

Your name is on my lips.
I breathe.

Living Word

I tune my heart to hear from You.

> ***Psalm 61:1–5***
> Hear my cry, O God,
>   listen to my prayer;
> from the end of the earth I call to you
>   when my heart is faint.

Lead me to the rock
    that is higher than I,
for you have been my refuge,
    a strong tower against the enemy.
Let me dwell in your tent forever!
    Let me take refuge under the shelter of your wings!
For you, O God, have heard my vows;
    you have given me the heritage of those who fear your name.

insecure

not being confident or assured, uncertain

The Language for Feeling Insecure

I looked around the room and everyone seemed so put together. They all seemed so strong. I saw their confidence and felt my insecurities. I sucked in my stomach and pulled my hair back into a slick ponytail. When it was my turn to speak, I stumbled through my introduction with nervousness. They gave pity laughter in response. The rest of the day I've been overanalyzing what I said. I secretly hoped they would forget their first impression of me. I feel insecure. I feel insecure about asking for help. I feel insecure about how much weight I've put on. I feel insecure when I don't know something I should know. I feel insecure that I haven't done enough. I am just good at hiding it. But if you saw inside of me, you would see it. You would see how quickly my soul grabs on to anything to find stability. You would see how I am scrambling to hide. If you look into my eyes long enough, you'll see my secret. You'll see straight into my insecure heart. You'll see just how lost I am in here.

I turn inward to find security by reciting good phrases, reading affirming words, or hanging on to praise from others. Becoming more assertive or aggressive helps to hide what feels fragile inside of me. Instead of fighting to get back up, I disengage from situations that puncture the little security I have. For a moment, I make space to feel my feelings and pay attention to my thoughts, my body, my story. I even listen to the lies that swarm my mind. This has happened before. My soul is free falling. I grab on to things to hold me up, but each thing turns to dust. My insecurities are a source of pain. There must be another way to live that won't leave me so anxious. A way that is marked by peace, love, and wholeness. My face turns to God even though I only want to focus on myself.

A Liturgy for When I Feel Insecure

Breathe in—*Lord God, help me . . .*
Breathe out—*rest into my belovedness.*

I feel insecure. I let myself feel what I feel.

I feel it in my body.

You meet me here. Right in the middle of my insecurities, You meet me.

Somewhere in my story, I believed that I had to be enough for myself or others to gain love, safety, or security. I had to garner my own power for the sake of protection. In some ways I failed at this. In some ways I succeed.

Search my heart, O God.

Reveal to me the ways my heart has been formed by fear.

You, God, are inviting me to be reshaped in love.

In Your kindness, You are stripping me of my ability to garner my own security.

My will may fail. My capacities may fail. My personality may fail. My body may fail. My performance may fail. My reputation may fail. Even my goodness may fail. But You, God, You will never fail.

All the things and people I have used to make me feel strong, I relinquish back to You.

In holy detachment, I refuse to use objects, relationships, or my own strength to make me feel strong.

I don't need to get out of my feelings; I need You to meet me in them.

As I feel my insecurities, I open my heart to You.

I believe that what I feel now is for my good.

I believe that You are here amid my circumstances, inviting me to walk forward in faith and walk inward with abiding trust.

I believe that even here, You want to secure my heart into my belovedness.

I touch my insecurities, but I am also touched by You.

This ache I feel is You healing me.

This shakiness is Your love strengthening me.

This fear is an invitation to be with You.

This is what it feels like to become whole. Your love collects my scattered pieces, gathers me up, molds me, and reforms me into the person You created me to be. Not one who must be enough to conquer any circumstance, but one tethered together by strong love.

God, give me courage to believe that the insecurity I feel is a part of my growth.

God, give me patience to endure the painful parts of my circumstances so I can fully live in peace.

God, grant me the wisdom to wade in my weaknesses long enough for Your Spirit to weld my heart together in love.

God, may this place I find myself today be a divine place where I welcome my fragileness and discover Your grace.

I don't have to be enough to be loved, safe, or secure.

Instead, I stand on my belovedness.

You are here. I bless Your name. My God, in You I place my hope.

My feelings of insecurity become the way in which Your grace meets me.

For this, I give You thanks. For this, my soul will praise Your name.

Living Word

I will listen to Your promises.

Psalm 40:1–4

I waited patiently for the LORD;
he inclined to me and heard my cry.
He drew me up from the pit of destruction,
out of the miry bog,
and set my feet upon a rock,
making my steps secure.
He put a new song in my mouth,
a song of praise to our God.
Many will see and fear,
and put their trust in the LORD.
Blessed is the man who makes
the LORD his trust,
who does not turn to the proud,
to those who go astray after a lie!

anxious

the general feeling of avoiding other important emotions

The Language for Feeling Anxious

I can't even recall when this feeling began. It just was. My body can't settle down. Everything itches. A slow-growing panic pulsing through me makes it difficult to breathe. I am anxious. I can manage many things, but not this. Fear races through me, and I can't rationalize, organize, or talk myself out of my escalated state of anxiety. Anxiety has a mind of its own. It is the boss. Trying to regain right thinking, a right posture, a right plan is exhausting. There is a war within me. A part of me has come to depend on my anxiety. While another part of me hates how much I am crippled by it. My wish is to just feel normal. To not have to deal with this. I wish things were different. I wish *I* was different.

I am compelled to manage my anxiety on my own. Letting others in is hard for me. It's embarrassing and hard trying to explain how I feel. Navigating other people's opinions and personal anecdotes adds another layer to my complex feelings. I just push through my anxiety, trying to stay ahead of the threat, but my anxiety so easily overtakes me. My voice, agency, and capacity to make decisions are gone. I withdraw because my feelings are so strong and so convincing. *Maybe this is just the way life is.* For a moment, I let my anxious feelings stay without fighting them or fleeing from them. I feel anxiety in my body. Fear is lodged inside of me. Anxiety twists and churns and disables me. I can't see an end. I am afraid these feelings will never change, and I will be stuck here. I cling to the hope that, even here, God can help me.

A Liturgy for When I Feel Anxious

Breathe in—*Jesus, help me . . .*
Breathe out—*enter into Your love.*

I feel anxious.

For a moment, I let myself feel.

I pay attention to where I feel anxiety in my body.

God, You are inviting me into something.

Something inside of me needs to be felt. Anxiety is a signal telling me that I am avoiding important emotions that I have not allowed myself to fully feel.

So I pause and make space for feelings that I have been suppressing.

Help me, God, to set aside the voices inside me that try to boss my feelings around, so that I may be attentive to my heart and what You have for me.

Search my heart, O God.

What are You inviting me to feel beneath my anxiety?

Whatever feeling I need to feel today and from my past, I allow myself to feel now.

I feel ________ (anger, sadness, grief, fear, disgust, etc.).

God, when have I felt this before in my story?

God, please do Your deep healing work in my life.

Help me, God, to be curious about my pain and the wounds that remain in me.

Help me, God, to be kind to myself as I enter and feel all that remains unfelt in my soul and story.

Gift me words for my heart.

God, this anxiety takes me on a journey that is rather painful, mysterious, and unknown to me.

Please, God, attend to my pain.

Please, in Your compassion, attend to my heart.

Please, God, in Your grace attend to the unhealed places within me.

You make space for my soul to be seen.

You want to finish writing the unfinished stories.

You pursue these sharp and stinging places within me.

I trust that my ache is the very place Your grace is healing me.

Feeling what I really feel is a sign of growth.

At the core of my being and at the core of my pain, You are with me.

With You, I don't have to manage or fix my anxiety, or make it stop. With You, I don't have to navigate it, avoid it, or dodge it. With You, I can be real about all that is good, hard, and still hurting within me.

With You is an ocean of compassion.

With You is a dwelling place of comfort.

With You I am made clean.

May this anxiety be what reminds my heart to pay attention to what is really going on in the deep waters of my soul. As I enter in, I make space to let my feelings flow. May I find You healing all the pain that I never allowed to be felt before.

Make sense of the shadows within me. Make known to me my heart. Make clear what seems confusing.

Even here, I discover new parts of me being reborn and I breathe.

May I see strength in me that I haven't experienced before.

I will know the healing of my soul is happening, not when my anxiety is gone, but when I am able to find gratitude for it along the way.

So, God, I thank You. Though my anxiety is painful, it is also a gift. It leads me to profound inner healing, hope, and ultimately closeness to You.

I will walk inward and onward, knowing that You, my Father, are not only with me, but leading me into the hidden places in my heart.

I lean on You. I limp on You. I love You and I am loved by You.

My God and my Savior, Amen.

Living Word

I want to hear what You have to say to me.

> ***Philippians 4:6***
> Do not be anxious about anything, but in everything by prayer and supplication with thanksgiving let your requests be made known to God.

stressed

having too much to do

The Language for Feeling Stressed

I don't have time for this. I made a mental checklist. One thousand things still remain. One thousand things that need my attention. I forgot to eat lunch today. Instead, fixing someone else's mistake took every spare second I had. From carrying the needs of others to canceling the appointment, I am just barely making it. At any moment it feels like everything will crack. If I don't keep going, things will fall apart, and that would be worse than what I feel right now.

It is hard to settle down. When I feel overwhelmed, I become stressed. Everything feels like it needs my immediate attention. Work, family, home, friendships, and all of the small extra things add up. The clock ticks away. My throat is closing in, my heart is racing, my chest is tightening. I feel anxious. I am trying to manage it all. Balancing my schedule, time, and obligations feels impossible. I quickly lean on my strength to make my stress go away or blame other people for it. Someone must be at fault for all the things I am left to do. Anger, resentment, and irritation build up inside of me. I lash out at people who don't deserve it.

To be really honest, I don't want to lay down the load I carry. Letting go seems like the harder task. I worry that if I let go, people and things will fall apart. This makes my burden even more unbearable. I let my feelings of stress stay. I try to listen to my body. I try to listen to my soul. I want a lot of things, but I want God more than anything. To be honest, I don't always act as if this is true. But the deepest part of me does want what God wants for me.

A Liturgy for When I Feel Stressed

Breathe in—*Spirit of the Living God, help me . . .*
Breathe out—*to listen.*

This is the place I find myself.

I feel stressed.

I allow myself to feel what I feel.

I feel where stress sits in my body.

God, I feel like I am being pulled apart.

My mind is going multiple directions. My heart is stretched from one place to the next. My body is here, but I am not present. I feel fear.

From this place, I open my heart to You.

I make space in my stress for Your love to meet me here.

If I listen and feed my stress, I only become more stressed.
If I listen to fear, I only become more impatient.
If I listen to the pressure, I only become more anxious.

God, I want to listen to You.
Within the voices of fear—I want to listen to Your voice of love.
Within all the pressure that is demanding my attention—I want to listen to Your voice of love.
Within the exhaustion of the weight I bear—I want to listen to Your voice of love.

The resolve of my stress comes when I don't seek to resolve my life on my own.

Here, God, I need You.

When everything and everyone is pulling at me, I call my soul to come back to You, God.

I have lost sight of my belovedness. I have lost the sense of my truest purpose. I have lost myself to the demands of the day. I have lost myself to the approval of others.

Here, now, God, may I find myself again.

I have been busy with many things and neglected the one thing that matters most.

The only thing I am responsible for right now is to listen to Your love, God.

You pull me into Yourself.

You piece me back together.

In my stress, fear, and hounding expectation—I will let You help me.
In the pressing circumstances—I will let You carry my load.
In all that must get done and in all I have left undone—I will let You gather me up.

Lord, as I sit at Your feet and listen to Your words—I find comfort.
Your Word promises peace (no matter what).
Your Word promises hope (no matter what).
Your Word promises protection (no matter what).
Your Word promises presence (no matter what).

In this, my heart takes comfort.
You don't demand that I do anything.
You invite me to come and receive love.

Please reorient my mind and heart to see You.
Please grant me the grace to ask for help as I need it.

From this place of abiding, please give me wisdom to do the next right thing in love.

Living Word

I trust the words You speak are true.

> ***Luke 10:38–42*** *NIV*
> As Jesus and his disciples were on their way, he came to a village where a woman named Martha opened her home to him. She had a sister called Mary, who sat at the Lord's feet listening to what he said. But Martha was distracted by all the preparations that had to be made. She came to him and asked, "Lord, don't you care that my sister has left me to do the work by myself? Tell her to help me!"
>
> "Martha, Martha," the Lord answered, ". . . Mary has chosen what is better, and it will not be taken away from her."

vulnerable

being exposed

The Language for Feeling Vulnerable

I said words that I can't get back. Words that were the truth but leave me trembling. I told my friend the full story and sat in silence. I'm so afraid my own words will betray me. I'm so worried she will learn the truth and leave me the way I've left myself all these years. I glance away but feel her eyes on me. I feel gutted. I don't know how to do this. Fear crawls up my rib cage like a spider. Anxiety, like a bungee cord, stretches and pulls across my chest. I've never felt more naked. My body shifts awkwardly. I feel so exposed, stupid, vulnerable. I badly want to escape my feelings. I feel powerless and painfully exposed. I think of ways to cover myself up again. I have to get out of here. Instead, I overexplain myself. I play small or shrink down. I feel so embarrassed. I want to wipe myself away. I can't believe how foolish I was to speak. My throat closes in and my heart pounds. I blush. I feel jittery.

I feel vulnerable because I am vulnerable. Being human is being vulnerable. It is what I am. But I don't know how to do this without wanting to disappear. I never want to feel this way again. Yet here I am. I am unable to stop this feeling. It is in me. It is a part of me. For a moment, I pause. I return to God.

A Liturgy for When I Feel Vulnerable

Breathe in—*Jesus . . .*
Breathe out—*I hide myself in Your love.*

I present my heart to You.

I feel vulnerable.

I pay attention to where it resides in my body.

God, truth has been exposed.
My real life is out there for others to see.

I am tempted to be defensive, overexplain, and protect myself.
I am tempted to dismiss, run away, or avoid those who are a threat.
I am tempted to wall up and hide.

There is a groaning in my spirit.

God, could it be that this feeling is the feeling of both death and life inside of me?

Something in me is dying while another thing is being born. I am encountering You here with me in this shaky place of releasing and receiving.

As my internal walls come down, my body agonizes, my spirit squirms, my heart contracts.

God, though this vulnerability is painful, I sense there is also good.

God, You invite me into healing.

You invite me into this rebirth. Although I want to hammer up new walls, close the gate, fortify my city, or find a back-road escape route, I refrain.

I let Your holy work happen in my heart.
I trust that as I am being seen, I am safe.
More than being rid of this pain, I want to be pruned in the image of Christ. I endure the uncomfortable sanctifying process of my soul for the sake of love.

God, I bring my bareness into Your belovedness.
I return to Your body on the cross hanging listless and limp.
You were exposed.
You were misunderstood.
You were propelled to endure pain because of love.
I find union with You here.

You know fragility.

You know weakness.

You know vulnerability.

No matter how crushed I feel—I trust that Your crushed body led to coming out of the grave clean.
No matter how tempted I am to cover—I trust that Your Spirit is at work uncovering truth inside of me.
No matter how scary it is to be seen—I trust You faced the scariest of things.

For it is in this tender place that the deep healing I need is found.

My feeling of vulnerability is actually a sign of growth.

God, give me courage to see myself clearly.
I lean into this vulnerable way of life.
It is the only way to love and be loved.
On the cross, Your weakness was wed to unfathomable strength.

I trust that You, my comforter and light, will lead me when the way is unknown.

My life is hidden in You, and with You there is safety.

I am becoming loved here.

I am becoming alive in new ways.

I am becoming and unfolding into who You created me to be.

I breathe through the birthing process.

Although this feeling aches within me, I also believe You are growing me. Your grace is sustaining me.

For this, I worship You. My heart will sing Your praise. My eyes will ever be on You.

Living Word

I will listen to You.

> ***Isaiah 53:5***
> But he was pierced for our transgressions;
> he was crushed for our iniquities;
> upon him was the chastisement that brought us peace,
> and with his wounds we are healed.

nervous

fearing that a good thing won't happen

The Language for Feeling Nervous

I turned in my application and, instantly, my insides went wild. I was fine until everything was out of my control and all that was left to do was wait. Then my anxiety kicked in. I want this so badly, and I can't do anything else to make it happen. Everything is out of my hands now, and I am left holding the possibility of joy or the possibility of loss. I don't have any control. I feel nervous. I don't like feeling this way. I think of things I can do to make the future go a certain way. *Maybe if I do this or that, I can obtain what I so desperately desire.* More research, more problem solving, more stuff, more creative thinking, more talking, more networking. When that doesn't work, I distract myself. There is even a small part of me that wants to abandon my desires entirely. My desires can be painful. It might be easier to walk away. My heart flutters around in my chest. I am full of energy. I am anxious that this good thing won't happen. I am afraid of what will come if things don't go the way I hope they will.

For a moment, I let my nervousness stay. I won't abandon my desires or try to control the situation either. I just let my feelings be. They are telling me something. I want a way forward that is easy and painless. But God may be doing something in my soul that I don't understand yet.

A Liturgy for When I Feel Nervous

Breathe in—*Jesus, brother and friend, remind me . . .*
Breathe out—*of Your goodness.*

God, I open my heart to You.

I feel nervous.

Help me notice where I feel my nervousness in my body.

Search my heart and help me recall when I have felt this kind of fear in my past.

As I wait for answers—I wait with You.
As I wait for the outcome—I wait with You.
As I wait in the sticky tension of what might or might not happen —I wait with You.

This is hard.

In my angst of not getting the good I desire, I come to You.
In my fear of missing out on something I long for, I come to You.
In the hope of something new, I come to You.

God, You are my ultimate good.
I may know in my head that You are good, but now, I am learning to experience, in my heart, that You actually are.

I accept that I don't have control over the circumstances before me.
I accept that most things are out of my hands.
Accepting this is not easy, but I present my palms bare before You.
I stay here with my heart vulnerably exposed before You.
I stand at the edge of my nervousness.
I am tethered between getting a good thing and the despair of not getting it.

Not getting it will cause me to encounter a deeper pain. A pain I don't want. A pain I am afraid of.

But I will trust in You.

You have not failed me, left me, or looked away from me.
I will trust that no matter what happens, You will uphold me.
You not only hold me, but I believe that in Your sovereignty You want what is best for my life.
I release what I think is right and trust that the road You lead me on is for my good.
I trust in You, my God and my Father.

Here, my soul is being strengthened.
Here, I bring my body, soul, and mind under Your wings of righteousness.
Here, I slowly believe that You, God, care about the good in my life more than I do.

You care about my desires even if You don't bring about the fulfillment of them.

If things go the way I hope, please Lord, help me to not leave Your side, but give You glory.

If things do not go the way I hope they will, Lord, please help me grieve, trust You, and bless Your name.

I thank You, even now, for it is through my nervousness that I am brought closer to You.

You meet me here, in my vulnerable hope.

Living Word

In return, I will listen to You.

> ***Isaiah 41:10***
> Fear not, for I am with you;
>   be not dismayed, for I am your God;
> I will strengthen you, I will help you,
>   I will uphold you with my righteous right hand.

overwhelmed

being buried under the weight of too many things

The Language for Feeling Overwhelmed

I worried when I missed the phone call. I need that information, and reaching an actual person is ridiculously hard. *Why are systems and people so incompetent?* My fear tightens around my chest like an imaginary rope. *I don't have time for this.* It isn't that the insurance information I need is too much. It is that I am already carrying so much. Today, everything feels heavy. My fear weighs me down. I'm just a single person, and I worry I can't and won't be enough. I worry bad things will come from my inability to carry it all. A lot has happened. A lot is happening. My body is moving, but my feelings can't keep up. I don't know how to process everything. I fear falling behind, and I get irritated at people for things that aren't their fault.

I feel overwhelmed. I feel the pressure to keep going. *Just keep going*, I tell myself. At the same time, I feel powerless and have been in survival mode for a while now. My overwhelm can turn into anxiety.

Limited resources and limited time stymie my efforts. I am afraid I won't have what it takes to process everything. I can't see an end or a way out. I don't seem to have a choice. I am tempted to disconnect. I shut down. Trusting God with all that I carry is difficult.

A Liturgy for When I Feel Overwhelmed

Breathe in—*Father God, help me . . .*
Breathe out—*lay down my burdens.*

I open my heart to You.

I feel overwhelmed.

I let myself feel what I feel.

My body holds my feelings.

Why soul, are you so afraid?

God,
Before I fight back, carry more, just keep going—I want to stop.
Before I disassociate, delve into self-pity, or run away—I desire to be still.
Before I do anything else—I'd like to hear from You.

God,
I don't listen to the constant demands stinging me like a windstorm.
I don't listen to the burning roar of the ferocious fire encroaching all around me.
I don't listen to the circumstances, expectations, needs, deadlines causing my soul's earth to shake.

God, in my overwhelm, I attend to Your whisper inviting me to come to You.

Help me distinguish Your voice from the voice of my flesh or the world.
The voices of my own flesh and the world bring with them panic and pressure. I will know Your voice because, like Elijah, when I listen to it, my heart will feel seen.

Give me the courage and curiosity to listen to Your voice.

Allow me to be compassionate and kind to myself as You are compassionate and kind to me.

You re-collect my heart by Your promises.
You say, *Do not fear for I am with you. I will be your refuge. Nothing can separate you from my love. Blessed are the pure in heart for they shall see God* (Isaiah 41:10; Psalm 91; Romans 8:39; Matthew 5:8).

One by one I lay my burdens down.

In holy detachment, I lay down all that You have not asked me to carry.

Help me lay down the load that isn't mine and hold delicately what is.
Help me give people the load that belongs to them—their pain, their consequences, their responsibilities, their emotions.
Help me surrender a future I can't control to You, the God who is fully in control.
Help me keep going, not out of fear, but from a desire to be faithful.

I slowly release the tight grip I have on my life.
I gently open the clasp I have on control.
I vulnerably believe that You care about my life more than I do.

I don't have to figure out my life on my own, rather, I get to come to You for the abundant life You promise.

God, may I walk with Your love at the center of my being.
Because of Your great love, I am sustained.
God, may I be faithful to what You have given me to carry today.

It is here, in my overwhelm, that I encounter Your humility.
You are a big God who cares about my little things.
You don't invite me to get out of my feelings, but to find You in them.

The thorn of my current circumstances and feelings is the pathway for Your love to meet me.

And for this, I give You thanks.
I will worship Your name all the days of my life.

Living Word

I trust that what You say is true.

> ***Matthew 11:28–30***
> Come to me, all who labor and are heavy laden, and I will give you rest. Take my yoke upon you, and learn from me, for I am gentle and lowly in heart, and you will find rest for your souls. For my yoke is easy, and my burden is light.

scared

fear that comes when something bad has happened or is happening

The Language for Feeling Scared

The car accident was entirely my fault. I went when the light was still red. I went because I was distracted. I slammed on my brakes. Crunch, crash, screams. I cursed. My kids cried. The man got out of his car belligerent. I apologized over and over. First to the man I hit and then to my kids.

The accident is hours behind me, but my body still feels the sting. I am scared of what is to come. I am afraid of the damage that must be undone. I worry about how much my mistake will cost us. Because I was the one at fault, I feel like I can't ask for help. I must take the consequences of my actions.

Part of me wants to run away—pretend nothing bad happened and just move on. Another part of me wants to fix everything. Fix the kids. Fix the car. Fix my failure. I want to manage my fear so I can feel safe again. I even want to defend myself even though I was at fault. For other people to see my mistakes is hard for me. Yet no matter what I do, I am still scared.

I let my fear stay for a moment without reacting. My body is trembling. My spirit is tied up. My eyes are shifting. What is really happening here? What do I really need to do? I listen. I wait. I want to understand my heart. I want safety, but I also don't want to always live in a state of high alert. I want another way to live that isn't bound by fear.

A Liturgy for When I Feel Scared

Breathe in—*Shepherd of my soul . . .*
Breathe out—*You are safe.*

God, I open my heart to You.

Grant me discernment to know if my fear is an indicator of real danger. Give me immediate help if evil is approaching.

In Jesus' name.

You are closer to me than this threat.
I trust that You walk with me.
In my fear, may I walk with You.

God, my feelings of being scared right now are a signal that my soul is asking for more care.

I listen with gentleness, curiosity, and courage.
I remember that in all things, Your desire is to love me.

God, I want to run through this valley.
I want a way out now.
I want an escape that is bearable.
I don't want pain for myself or others I love.
Yet, God, You have not allowed my fear to come to an end yet.
You have not removed the threat.
You have not changed the circumstances.
You have not made this easy.
You have not granted me a passageway out of my pain, but through it.

In Your will, You have allowed what has happened to happen.
I wish there were another way.
A way without fear, enemies, danger, darkness, or death.

But, God, You have given me this story.
You have appointed me to this moment in time.
You have prepared me for this juncture from all the past journeys I have been through.
So with reluctance and fear and hesitation, I turn the dependence I have on myself over to dependence on You.

What do I have left, but You?

You rescue me through a relationship with You.
It is by love You make space for me at the table.
It is by love You tend to every nuance of my needs.
It is by love You abundantly and absurdly and recklessly pour out Your grace.

My cup overflows.

Enemies remain enemies.
Darkness remains darkness.
Danger remains danger.
But I sit at Your table and receive Your love for me.

I stay at this table with every scary thing I feel.
Here, You serve me.
Here, I drink from the cup of Your love, not from the fountain of my fear. Here, I find nourishment from the bread of Your body broken for me. Here, I receive care—body, soul, and mind.

No trauma can tear me apart from Your affection for me.
The more and more I come here, the more and more healing I find.
This dwelling place is a home for me not to be held hostage to fear, but a place for me to find safety in the midst of it.
As I stay, without realizing it, I am actually moving forward.

I am being healed.
Yes and amen.

Living Word

God, I am listening.

Psalm 23:4–6

Even though I walk through the valley of the shadow of death,
    I will fear no evil,
for you are with me;
    your rod and your staff,
    they comfort me.

You prepare a table before me
    in the presence of my enemies;
you anoint my head with oil;
    my cup overflows.
Surely goodness and mercy shall follow me
    all the days of my life,
and I shall dwell in the house of the LORD
    forever.

desperate

feeling that nothing you can do is enough

The Language for Feeling Desperate

I feel an uncontrollable urge to reach out to you. I know you said you needed space, but the more space I give you, the more afraid I feel. I need you to need me. Groveling is the lowest a human can go. It actually feels inhumane. But here I am, needing your affection. Here I am, desperate to get you back. If you take me, then I feel like I'll be okay. I feel awful. I'll do anything not to feel this way. If that means begging, I'll do it.

What have I become? I feel desperate. This feeling scares me. I don't want to be in this place. Inside of me there is anger, despair, and sadness too. I never imagined giving parts of myself in order to be accepted. I am tempted to take, grab, lie, cheat, demand, beg, scream, scheme, or manipulate to gain some sort of control. My feelings have complete reign over me. Self-pity can consume me. I want everyone to know how terrible my life is, so I call attention to my misery to get consolation. Feeling sorry for myself nurses my wound but doesn't take away my pain. I feel desperate.

Right now, even though it is excruciating, I let my feelings stay. I listen to my body. The ache is so deep that breathing is painful. When will this feeling go away? Everything seems hard. I want a way out, but every turn looks like more and more pain.

A Liturgy for When I Feel Desperate

Breathe in—*Father God . . .*
Breathe out—*You love me even here.*

I feel desperate.

I feel it in my body.

Search my heart and my story, O God.

When have I felt this way before?

I open my heart to You.

God, my soul is pleading for more care.

I remind myself, now, that the greatest intention You have for my life is to love me.
Even if I don't feel this, I try to believe it.
I am finite. I am human. I am here.

God, You invite me to pause.

I don't have to get out of my feelings or circumstances on my own.
I don't have to panic or claw my way out.

I let myself feel what I feel.

I don't have to turn in on myself or run away.
I don't have to give another person all the power.
I don't need to fight my feelings.
I don't need to do that anymore.

But this is what I can do.

God, I can come to You.

I can follow my desperate feelings to the deeper story of my pain.
I can be open and remember the helplessness I felt.
I bring my body, mind, soul, and heart into this place.

Breath by breath.
I am here.
Even now, this is what I can control.
I can let You love me.
I can move my body toward that which is beautiful, true, good, and right.
I can open my fearful soul to You.

God, I feel stuck.
I feel alone.
I feel gutted.

I feel the darkness.
I feel scared.

It is hard to breathe.

You, Jesus, know desolation.

You, Jesus, know loneliness.

You, Jesus, know darkness.

You, Jesus, know fear.

I feel comfort knowing You know my pain.

You will not leave me here, but everything that is broken will be made whole. You are doing this even now.

I trust You are near.
I trust You are with me.
I trust that, somehow and some way, You will heal this agonizing feeling.

I fall on You.

I breathe.
I receive Your love.
I receive my story, even with all its pain.

I trust even now, as I feel my ache, that this is the way You are healing me.

I breathe.

Let this be my worship, O God.

Living Word

Help me listen to You.

> ***Luke 22:42–44***
> "Father, if you are willing, remove this cup from me. Nevertheless, not my will, but yours, be done." And there appeared to him an angel from heaven, strengthening him. And being in agony he prayed more earnestly; and his sweat became like great drops of blood falling down to the ground.

worried

concerned over a specific area of your life (money, health, work, relationships, time)

The Language for Feeling Worried

I swiped my card and anxiously waited. A blaring beep signaled there was an error. I was worried this might happen. I pretended to be confused. "Let me try again," I said, knowing that *trying again* wouldn't make a difference. Re-swipe. I chatted with the checker while my throat was closing in. I told her that it was a new card and this has been happening a lot. But I knew it wasn't the card's mistake. I knew we were past our limit, maxed out, in debt, broke. The error message raised an alarm again. I felt my hands sweating. I searched my purse for another card. Nothing. I assured the teenager bagging my groceries that I would be right back. I knew I wouldn't. I left in a panic. I left with a shame cloud growing over me as though a storm were coming. More than anything, I was worried. I was concerned about what the financial state of my life would mean. This one fear quickly turned into many, and I feared losing everything.

Worry consumes me. If it isn't our finances, it's the weird blemish on my neck or the strange sound coming from the vent. How many nights have I lain awake pacing the hallways of my mind, worried about tomorrow and the day after that? How many times have I recounted a conversation? How many times have I checked and rechecked the internet, the temperature, the text? Too many to count.

For a moment, I let my worry stay. I let it take up space without trying to negotiate with it or tame it. I let it fill all of me without fighting back. I feel alone, but I know God is with me. It makes no sense that I can know He is with me but also feel consumed by relentless worries. I can't reconcile what my mind believes to be true about God and the fear that consumes my heart.

A Liturgy for When I Feel Worried

Breathe in—*Lord God, help me . . .*
Breathe out—*walk with You.*

I feel worried.

For a moment, I let myself feel what I feel.

I feel worried in my body.

Search my heart, O God, and help me see the part worry has played in my story.

God, I want control over the future.
I am afraid.
I want things to go a certain way.
I want a painless way.

I try to be attentive to every detail.
This constant vigilance has left my soul exhausted.
I am anxious I will make a mistake, do things wrong, be the cause of another person's pain, not be enough, or not know enough.

But, Lord, I will not listen to the great temptress of worry.
She will only lead me astray.
She will lure me into future places You have not invited me to go.

I am fearful.
I let myself fall into my deepest fear.
I am really afraid of pain.

What if I can't stop the bad thing from happening?

At the end of every worst-case scenario is pain.
I work so hard to protect myself and others from such an outcome.
Yet You, God, walked into pain, not from it.

You faced the cross.
You faced death.
You faced fear.
You faced separation from relationships You loved.

With courage, You stepped toward the very thing that caused Your body to tremble and break.

With conviction, You kept walking even in the face of great fear.

With humility, You looked to Your Father for love.

With faith, You faced abandonment.

For You, pain was not the worst-case scenario; eternal death and separation from us was.

Here I am, worried and afraid.

By Your grace may I come under Your arms of protection.
May I find courage to step toward that which causes my body to tremble and break—as You did.

May I find conviction to keep walking even when fears abound—as You did.
May I find humility to keep my eyes on my Father's love—as You did.
May I find faith to face losing everything I hold dear—as You did.

Pain is not my greatest enemy; living a life separated from Your love is.
With You and in You, I have everything my soul needs—You.

I may lose my wealth; I may lose my property; I may lose my power; I may lose my health; I may lose my reputation; I may lose my loved ones; I may lose my life, but my God, You will never lose me.

The only way I find resolve for my worry is to walk through it with Your love. I don't need to rid myself of worry. I need to go through it vulnerably with You.

Help me believe that I am a detail You watch over with great attention and care. Help me attend to the life You have given me in this present moment.

Help me stay here, in this hour, in this second, in this breath—with You.

Even though my feelings of worry are hard for me, I give thanks, because through them I am learning that they make a way for me to meet with You.

Living Word

I will listen to You.

> ***Matthew 6:31–34*** *NLT*
> Don't worry about these things, saying, "What will we eat? What will we drink? What will we wear?" These things dominate the thoughts of unbelievers, but your heavenly Father already knows all your needs. Seek the Kingdom of God above all else, and live righteously, and he will give you everything you need.
>
> So don't worry about tomorrow, for tomorrow will bring its own worries. Today's trouble is enough for today.

guilty

fearing that punishment awaits you for a crime or wrongdoing you have committed

The Language for Feeling Guilty

I lied. It wasn't a big lie. I didn't even straight-up lie. But I did lead others to believe something that wasn't true. I skirted around honesty as though I were allergic to it. I was afraid of being found out, so I brushed past vulnerability. Now I am left with guilt sticking to me. No amount of justification and rationalization can peel it off me.

My guilt feels all knowing and all powerful. I so badly want my guilt gone. I hide, I cover, I lie. I do good as a way to feel good. I dodge direct questions, avoid conflict, or feel the need to constantly justify my actions. I beat myself up with blame, unable to escape my own self-condemnation. I can't see a way through the situation. This is hard for me.

I let my guilt simmer inside of me for a moment. I let it stay without trying to manage it. It is so uncomfortable to feel. I have worked relentlessly to separate myself from my guilt. I just want to feel better, but I pause now. I slow down. I let myself feel what I feel before jumping to action. My heart rate increases. I feel scattered, hurried, and afraid. I have a hard time thinking clearly. I so badly want to be free. I pray.

A Liturgy for When I Feel Guilty

Breathe in—*God, my Father . . .*
Breathe out—*You love me even here.*

I feel guilty.

Search my heart, O God.

When in my story have I felt this feeling before?

God, help me listen.
Right now, all I can hear is my guilt.
It plagues me.

I am afraid of being found out.
I am afraid of punishment or condemnation.

God, help me know if this guilt is from You or from another source.

I place my hand to my head.

I want to know if I am feeling false guilt.
Am I trying to keep laws and rules that You didn't ask me to obey?
If I have not actually broken a command of Yours, this guilt is not from You, but from a false god in my life.

God, if I did something that is truly wrong, I seek forgiveness.
Help me accept forgiveness.
I have sinned against You or another.
God, forgive me for my wrong.
Yet even as I speak these words, conflict is provoked within me.
I want to atone for my own guilt.

Be it pride or vanity or greed or self-righteousness, deep within my will, it is incredibly hard to accept that I can't save myself.
I want to prove myself.
I want to restore myself.
I hate that I can't.

I place my hand to my heart and receive Your forgiveness for my sins.

God, You invite me to feel my fear.
Guilt, at its core, is about fear.
I have been afraid of punishment.
I have been worried about being known for who I really am and what I have really done.
I have been anxious that if the truth came out, I wouldn't be loved.

I feel the deep vulnerability that I am not who I want to be.
This is painful.
When fear emerges, help me greet this feeling with gentleness instead of hiding.
Let fear be what leads me to You instead of lying, covering, and pretending.

Lord, no fear, no guilt, no pride, no crime committed can separate me from Your love.

I place my hand upon my gut.

Your love lives at the core of my existence.

God, help me receive Your forgiveness.

You are right here, in kindness, relieving me of my need to earn, prove, or get forgiveness by my own strength.
I take in Your grace, delight, and kindness.

When I am afraid, help me react by turning to You instead of to myself.

The only thing I am truly guilty of is not receiving Your love.

I hold open my hands.

I open my heart.

Even here, I can give thanks because it is through this fear that I am able to experience Your grace and communion.

Living Word

God, Your child is listening.

> ***Romans 8:38–39***
> For I am sure that neither death nor life, nor angels nor rulers, nor things present nor things to come, nor powers, nor height nor depth, nor anything else in all creation, will be able to separate us from the love of God in Christ Jesus our Lord.

3

anger

Angry—a strong feeling of annoyance, displeasure, or hostility

Agitated—feeling repeatedly bothered

Frustrated—anger when obstacles interfere with what you need or want

Resentful—feeling ill-will from being mistreated

Numb—the feeling of not feeling

Skeptical—questioning the honesty of a person's actions or intentions

Furious—feeling out-of-control anger

Lazy—not wanting to attend to the life you've been given

Jealous—wanting what other people have

Annoyed—irritated by the needs and actions of others

Failure—the feeling of not being who you want to be

Exhausted—deep tiredness that fuels anger

Betrayed—the result of someone violating your trust

angry

a strong feeling of annoyance, displeasure, or hostility

The Language for Feeling Angry

I want to be anywhere but here. I am about to lose control. I can tell. I feel anger boiling within me. It is prowling like a prisoner right behind my rib cage, eager to get out. I try to simmer it down. I try to drink water, take some space, and walk away. But I can't escape myself. I can't cut myself off from my convictions. I can't dismember my body from my feelings. I'm mad about many things. My anger, like a tornado, snatches up everything wrong I see. Everything swirls together. I haven't been heard. I haven't been seen. I haven't had a place to stand up and tell my side of the story. It isn't right or fair or okay. My soul spews. I can't sit. I can't process it. I can't think straight. I am coming undone. I feel so angry. I want to shout harsh words, entertain evil thoughts, or punish other people. I am gripped by my anger. I want control. I implode on myself. I so easily become the victim of my anger. I lose myself to my feelings. My anger takes over me. I let it. My anger scares even me.

For a moment, I don't try to manage my anger, but just feel it. It consumes me. I feel helpless. I also feel other feelings. I feel deeply hurt, betrayed, confused, misunderstood, invisible.

Exploding or imploding can't be the only way out of what I feel. There must be another way that doesn't cause greater damage than what has already been done. I want to do a lot of things with my anger. Though there are parts of me that want to bring harm or vindication or revenge or justification, ultimately, I don't want to destroy myself or another. I know those actions won't bring me freedom but destruction. How do I hold on to anger when anger is needed, but not use it as a weapon to bring harm?

A Liturgy for When I Feel Angry

Breathe in—*Jesus, companion and friend . . .*
Breathe out—*help me be wise.*

God, here I am.

I feel angry.

I feel it in my body and trace it in my story.

Even in my resistance, please help me do the best "right thing" in love.

I resist feeding my anger with anger.
I resist picking up the weapon of my tongue or the force of my hand to resolve my feelings.
I resist pushing my anger down, pretending it isn't there, or turning it against myself.

You say, Let not the sun go down on my anger.
You have not commanded me to reconcile with my offender immediately but have invited me to be *with* my anger through the day and night.

I want to be honest with myself.
I know in the darkness of my anger, I can make up stories that may not be true.
I can imagine plans for harm.
I can believe lies that shape my thinking and behavior.

Search my heart, O God.

As I stay with my anger, Lord, lead me to my wounds.
Bring my pain to the light so anger doesn't rot my bones.
O good counselor, help me process my pain in a way that brings full resolve.

You have given me anger as a gift. It allows me to see my heart, reality, right, and wrong. May I yield this gift as an offering of service and not self-righteousness or self-condemnation.

In my anger I turn my attention to You, Jesus.
I turn my combustible chest to You.
I bring my frustration, hostility, and hurt to You.
For You, God, are always turned toward me.

I stretch open my frustrated soul.
I stretch open my pain.
I stretch open my ache.

No one can fully handle my anger but You.
You are not surprised by it.
You don't reject me or come undone by my pain, but You reveal my heart to me.

Instead, You pull me in.

You know anger too.
You've felt it, expressed it, and received the wrath of others.
You rebuked. You got frustrated. You flipped tables.

You know the anger of man and have not raged back, but instead, You healed.

When Mary was angry at You for not being back in time to save her brother, You tended to her pain. When Peter cut off the soldier's ear in anger, You healed. When they murdered You on the cross, You forgave.

You take people's anger.

This is what You do.

Help me to speak, shout, or scream the truth—in love.
Help me find a way forward.
Help me, O God, to be wise with my words and actions.
Help me heal that I may be fully free to love.

Even amid this burning feeling, I give You thanks because You move toward me. Even here, I find comfort in knowing that You care about my anger, hurt, and pain.

Living Word

I will listen to You.

> ***Ephesians 4:25–27***
> Therefore, having put away falsehood, let each one of you speak the truth with his neighbor, for we are members one of another. Be angry and do not sin; do not let the sun go down on your anger, and give no opportunity to the devil.

agitated

feeling repeatedly bothered

The Language for Feeling Agitated

My children put me on edge. My mom's tone of voice on the phone is still bugging me. There is stuff accumulating on every surface, and I feel my agitation growing. People everywhere somehow forgot how to drive. I've been so bothered recently. I get bothered that I'm bothered.

The slightest touch, the repetitive sounds, the nagging needs, the constant motion around me, the insensitivity of others gets under my skin. I am trying my best not to lose my temper. I am doing everything I can to stay calm. But I am on the defense and trying to protect my space. I feel like a pressure cooker ready to blow. My body feels hot. I take everything in all at once. Things keep piling up. Everything is closing in on me. Everything is out of place. Everything is wrong. I don't like feeling this way. I need and want someone to blame because I can't be at fault for how I feel. I want a way out. I want to run away. If I can just control the situation, I'll be okay. I scream. I belittle. I shame. I push through the anger sitting on my chest by hurrying, stressing, and plowing through it. I so easily become a victim of my feelings. I can withdraw, shut down, disconnect.

For a moment, I let myself feel what I feel without reacting. My throat is tight, my skin feels itchy, and even my shoulders are high. In some ways, my body feels like it has betrayed me. I have a headache. I want a way through this that doesn't cause more pain. I am tired. I am tired of feeling this way. I want healing.

A Liturgy for When I Feel Agitated

Breathe in—*Jesus, Jesus, Jesus . . .*
Breathe out—*You see me.*

I feel agitated.

I let myself feel what I feel.

This feeling locates itself in my body, and I notice where it is.

God, I open myself to You.

At some point, I felt missed or went unseen.
My soul didn't get what it needed.
My agitation is making me even more agitated.
Reveal to me what feeling I feel beneath my agitation.
Where is my anger rooted?

What do I need?

God, I need space.
Here and now, I need it.
I breathe.

God, when others or I haven't, You attend to my soul.
I shift my heart to You.
I take one step toward You rather than taking another step toward bitterness or resentment.

God, I take up space.
I have limited space, but in Your presence, God, there is limitless space. You make room for me.
I breathe.

My soul is unsettled within me.
My heart has been missed and gone unseen.
My body aches to be known and loved.
My anger is inviting me to see the unresolved pain I carry.

With You, there is room for my pain to be exposed.
You give me expansive space.
Space as far as the stars and as far as the seas.
I breathe.

You make room for me to feel and hurt and ache and be angry.
In Your house there are no rules.
You let me make a mess, keep on my shoes, toss my things on the floor.
I breathe.

Here, I am loved.
O good counselor, attend to my soul, pain, and story.
Attend to the sadness or neglect or loneliness that lives beneath the surface.
Give me comfort now for the comfort I didn't receive in my past.
You receive my needs, desires, disdain, reluctance, expectations.
You receive all of me.

Forgive me for when I have brought harm to others or myself with my anger.
Forgive me for lashing out before listening.
Forgive me for when I may have lost control.

Help me attend to what matters most right now.
Many things are important.
But meeting here with You, O Lord, is what my soul needs most of all.

God, in this space, You attend to my deepest needs.

You, Lord, are patient with me even when I am impatient with myself.
You pour cool water onto my hot heart.

With all my agitation, help me.

Gift me with grace to be curious about my heart and the ways You are at work to heal me.

Gift me with Your kindness.

Gift me with Your compassion for my shortcomings and the shortcomings of others.

Give me strength to endure what You've asked me to carry.
Give my soul enough space to sustain me when I feel strangled.

For even in my agitation, I can touch Your grace. Your grace is sufficient for the story You have given me.

Lord, have mercy on me.

Living Word

I incline my heart to hear from You.

> ***Ecclesiastes 7:9***
> Be not quick in your spirit to become angry,
> for anger lodges in the heart of fools.

frustrated

anger when obstacles interfere with what you need or want

The Language for Feeling Frustrated

Nothing seems to be going my way today. I feel like time is against me. From traffic lights to incompetent people, I am bothered that I can't get done what needs to be done. Poorly run systems, others not listening, the actions or lack of actions by others, or a messy house set me off because they get in the way of me getting to the one thing I need—a moment to relax.

I am more than irritated. I am frustrated. In a moment, my anger can feel so strong. If I want something done, I have to use force. Instead of lashing out, I shut down. My anger turns cold inside of me, and I feel powerless. I can become passive aggressive, resentful, or critical. My frustration may not be expressed externally, but I'm fuming on the inside.

My chest, face, and throat almost burn.

I don't want to harm myself or others. I don't want to hurt people. I don't. I can't seem to love well, which is my deepest desire. Sometimes I don't know what else to do to be heard and get what I need.

There must be another way.

A Liturgy for When I Feel Frustrated

Breathe in—*Holy Spirit . . .*
Breathe out—*console me.*

I open my heart to You.

I feel frustrated.

I feel it in my body.
God, my feelings of frustration are a signal that my soul is asking for more care.

Search my heart, O God.

Reveal to me the root of this feeling and the pain it stems from.

Allow me to see if there is pain in my story that You are intending to heal through the anger that I feel right now.

I want to be with You as You are with me.

God, my frustration only seems to grow.

There are things I want and need.

Sometimes I feel guilty for having desires.

I don't want to be motivated or moved by guilt or shame, but by love.

My desires and the obstacles getting in the way of those desires are in conflict.
I feel friction.
Heat on the inside of me.
Heat on the outside of me.

Lord, hear my needs as a prayer.

Help me be curious about what I really want. Help me be curious about what I really need. Help me be gentle with myself and others.
Father, forgive me if my frustration has led to sin.
Help me also move toward forgiving those who have sinned against me.

Help me listen to my own heart with kindness and courage. God, help me remember that the greatest intention You have for my life is to love me.

You do not turn Your face from me, but to me.

You listen intently to my desires, wants, and needs.
You bear my burdens.
You are with me, here.
My feelings are cooled by Your faithfulness.

More than anything, what I really want is communion with You.
I want You to look upon my life with pride and gladness.
I want to love generously and graciously.
I want my life to be an offering to You.

Even here, I am reminded of my belovedness.
From this place of frustration, Your love invites me into healing, freedom, and greater peace.
My anger is soil for Your grace to tend to my soul.
For this, I give You thanks.

Living Word

Your words are the words of life.
I will listen.

Ephesians 4:15
Rather, speaking the truth in love . . .

resentful

feeling ill-will from being mistreated

The Language for Feeling Resentful

The other day when my husband was out of town and my schedule was already maxed out, someone dropped off their kids for me to watch. I was already drowning and felt so dismissed. I am the fallback person. I pick up the loose ends. I'll make the meal, plan the event, remember to get the ice. People know I'll say yes, and I do. I want to love well, but I have been hurt. Resentment festers in me. I feel it brewing. I can feel it simmering. Somehow my anger strengthens me. I lick my bitterness; it tastes sweet. I sometimes get satisfaction in nurturing my displeasure. I don't want to be this kind of a person. As much as I am angry and hurt, I don't want my pain to poison me.

I confess that my mind takes me down a dark road of revenge. In my suffering, I want others to suffer too, and I become a vengeful victim. I confess I am also tempted to turn my suffering inward. I have a tendency toward self-hate or pushing down my true feelings. I feel frustrated because I *should* be able to handle my life. I think something must be wrong with me for feeling this way. My resentment turns to bitterness and even entitlement.

For a moment, I allow my feelings of resentment to stay. I resist moving to any sort of action or minimizing what I feel. I let resentment reside in me without trying to resolve it. I feel it and my body tightens. I let all that is with me be as it is. I am aware that I have pain. Using power or assuming powerlessness have not resolved my wounds, but rather further increased them. There must be another way through this.

A Liturgy for When I Feel Resentful

Breathe in—*Jesus, Jesus, Jesus . . .*
Breathe out—*help me bless.*

God, I open my heart to You.

I feel resentment.

I feel it in my body, and it gnaws at me.

Search my heart, O God, that I may see the ways resentment has shaped my story.

Where did it come from?

God, I was wronged.
I have been violated and it isn't right.
I wasn't cared for, noticed, or considered.
My anger has turned bitter in my soul.

God, You invite me to feel my anger, but not to indulge it.
You invite me to pass through it, but not to become entangled in it.

I am in conflict between who I am and who I want to be.

Allow me to set aside false shame so that I can see the roots of my resentment and the real pain that resides there.

This pain is real.

I allow myself to feel it now.

Sometimes it is hard to feel, see, and name.

But, You, Lord, see my heart. You see my ache. You see the ways I have struggled.

You see what others can't see.

You, Lord, know what it is like to struggle too.
You were hurt.
You were taken advantage of.
You were mistreated.

I come into Your love and find comfort in knowing I am not alone here.

Help me be curious about my own heart and story.
Help me be kind to and compassionate toward my stinging soul.
Help me find release from the resentment that rattles me.

And if I can't find relief, Lord, I pray I can receive Your grace for the things I can't change. I need You here. You see me and all I have done.

I trust that You are healing me even through this ache.
I trust that Your Spirit is deeply at work in my heart.
I trust that You are penning a story from anger to freedom.

With Your grace, help me bless those who have hurt me.
God, help me not to feed my anger with more anger, but please feed my anger with Your love.

I open my anger to You.

I open my heart to the cross.

I breathe.
I find comfort here.
I borrow Your prayer now, "Father, forgive them, for they know not what they do" (Luke 23:34).

Lord, hear my prayer.

Living Word

I want to hear from You.

> ***Romans 12:17–21***
> Repay no one evil for evil, but give thought to do what is honorable in the sight of all. If possible, so far as it depends on you, live peaceably with all. Beloved, never avenge yourselves, but leave it to the wrath of God, for it is written, "Vengeance is mine, I will repay, says the Lord." To the contrary, "if your enemy is hungry, feed him; if he is thirsty, give him something to drink; for by so doing you will heap burning coals on his head." Do not be overcome by evil, but overcome evil with good.

numb

the feeling of not feeling

The Language for Feeling Numb

We moved. It wasn't a move I wanted. I packed boxes and parts of my heart away. I have felt so little recently. It isn't that nothing has happened. It's that too much has. A cold layer is living on the upper part of my chest. I can't access my emotions. I don't want to access them. This shield protects me. I can't crack open my heart. I am worried that I don't actually care. In all I have had to let go of and all that I've endured, I wonder if there is a part of me that just doesn't care anymore. I go through the motions of everyday life, but I feel a little apathetic, indifferent, and numb.

I am tempted to stay busy. If I can just keep going, I won't have to feel the feelings I actually feel inside. I keep myself moving constantly. I have a full schedule, an active life. My busyness allows me to stay detached from my body, story, and pain. I also want to withdraw. I pull back and inward. I isolate myself. But when I am alone, I am drawn toward distractions because I want to keep my pain away. I slowly become detached from my own heart. Things like getting lost in a book, social media, or task management keep me safe from unwanted feelings. For a moment, I stay with my feeling of numbness. I often dismiss it, but for a moment, I give it my attention. I listen to my body. It never lies. I have a dull ache. I am tempted to manage my feelings alone. But more than anything, I want to be with God.

A Liturgy for When I Feel Numb

Breathe in—*Jesus, Savior and shepherd . . .*
Breathe out—*I want to be with You.*

I feel numb.

I allow myself to feel what I feel.

I open my heart to You, God.

Search my heart and the story of numbness in my life.

I have slid a lid over my heart as a way to survive.
This place of not feeling seems safe.
There is a part of me that intentionally puts up a stop sign when my emotions start to peek through.

You see me trying to protect my heart.
You see every part of my story.
You see what I am going through.

Even as I feel disconnected, I want to be connected to You, God.
Perhaps You have something for me here.

Perhaps there is a way through hard things that doesn't require me to close down my heart entirely.

With Your gentleness, help thaw out my heart a little at a time.
Whatever it is I need to feel, I open my heart to You.
Do I need to stay numb?

Do I need to grieve?
Do I need to feel the mess of my complicated heart?

I ask that You slowly turn the light on in my soul.

Perhaps I am afraid of my real feelings.
It's possible that I am uncertain of how deep they go.
Maybe I am worried that once I feel what I feel, I will lose control.

God, help me see how close You really are to me.

Help me know I don't have to protect myself or others all on my own. Help me peel back the layers of my soul and feel the safety I have in You. Help me not to depend on my ability to be strong more than I depend on You.

God, for the ways You have given me protection from my pain with numbness, I give You thanks.

Slowly remove the cast placed around my heart when the time is right. As I unfold what is under my feeling of numbness, I ask for Your grace. I ask for kindness. I ask for courage and curiosity to see my soul as it really is. Help me find words for what I feel. One word at a time. Let each one be a prayer that You delightfully receive—*I don't even know what I feel. I don't feel anything. I don't want to feel. I have to be strong. I feel stuck. It all feels like too much.*

Awaken me to Your love even here.

Lord, may I know that this feeling of numbness is a gift from You. I receive it in faith knowing that You intend good for my life. Your grace meets me here and guides me to Your love.

Even when I don't understand my own heart, You do.

To You, I lift up my soul. To You, I come. To You, I entrust my life.

Living Word

God, I am listening.

> ***Ephesians 5:13-14***
> But when anything is exposed by the light, it becomes visible, for anything that becomes visible is light. Therefore it says,
>
> "Awake, O sleeper,
>   and arise from the dead,
>   and Christ will shine on you."

skeptical

questioning the honesty of a person's actions or intentions

The Language for Feeling Skeptical

Someone with authority spoke. I heard words but didn't believe them. They sounded convincing and confident, but my soul was flashing a warning sign. It didn't make sense. I question myself. I question my sanity. I look back at the facts. Something isn't adding up. I let it go, but I can't fully forget. Something just isn't right. I heard your words, but I hear mine also. I feel skeptical. I am tempted to attack. I want to lash out at a person or institution. I have a tendency to enter every scenario defensively. People tend to be untrustworthy.

I am also tempted to turn inward. Because others can't be trusted, I can only trust myself. My perspective is the only right perspective. I slowly step away from relationships, community, systems, and institutions because I have such a hard time trusting anyone. My gut is usually right. I can sense and see things that others can't. I refuse to be gullible or negligent. But I am often left lonely. Oftentimes I feel angry, and I don't fully know why.

Even now, before I react to my feelings, I just need to feel my feelings. I let my skepticism stay without trying to feed or fight it. My heart rate increases, and I notice I'm sweating. It's hard for me to slow down. If I am wrong or if I am right, either way, I don't want to live always questioning everyone and everything. I want peace. I am trying to protect myself, but I'm also left feeling agitated.

A Liturgy for When I Feel Skeptical

Breathe in—*Father God . . .*
Breathe out—*help me trust in You.*

I feel skeptical.

I open my heart to You.

God, is this a familiar feeling in my life?

You have given me the gift of intuition.
I know in my gut if something or someone is safe.
But at some point in my story, my discernment became disordered.
Instead of being able to discern safe from unsafe, everything and everyone became dangerous to some degree.

Out of my pain, anger manifests itself as skepticism.

You, God, invite me to come back to You for safety.
People who were meant to love me have in some way let me down.
But, God, You have never failed me.

I don't want to abandon my gut instincts, but I don't let them rule me either.

You call me into discernment.
I need Your help knowing what is dangerous and what requires faith.
God, before I lunge toward accusations, I bring my questions and concerns to You.

Before I turn inward, only trusting myself, I come to You.
Before I trust my judgment alone, I look to You.
Before I reach for reasons to run away, I return to You for the safekeeping of my life and those I love.

Christ, be my compass.

I still my soul.

I lay my heart beside calm waters.
From this at-home place, I let my feelings come under Your guidance.

Lord, help me resist letting skepticism alone lead me.
I don't have to resolve, protect, or defend others or myself all on my own.
I relinquish what I think I know for that which I don't know.

God, help me trust You before I trust my skepticism.

Help me know that just because I have a thought, it doesn't mean that's what I think.
Help me speak when I need to speak.
Help me know when to stay and when to walk away.
Help me honor You above all things.

God, heal what was wounded in me so that this gift You have given me can be used as an offering and not as a shield.

Lord, hear my prayer.

Living Word

I will listen to Your words of life.

> ***Proverbs 3:5–6*** *NASB*
> Trust in the LORD with all your heart
> and do not lean on your own understanding.
> In all your ways acknowledge Him,
> and He will make your paths straight.

furious

feeling out-of-control anger

The Language for Feeling Furious

"How can you leave us? You promised to love us. You promised to always stay." I typed those words ferociously. The man who was like family left, and I am losing myself. My body feels wrecked. My heart is pounding with rage. I feel like I am really losing my mind. I am tempted to be physically violent. I just want this feeling out of me. Slamming a door, driving wildly, screaming, or destroying something feels like the only release for the outrage I feel. I use rage as a way out of my pain. I turn my anger inward. I want to bring harm to my own body. I am so desperate for relief. In the secret places of my heart, I have planned or imagined evil to come to another. Rage can move me to apathy because I have a hard time believing this pain will ever end.

For a moment, I let this feeling consume me without moving to action. I let it stay without reacting or trying to figure it out. Feeling my anger is painful and powerful. It scares me. I feel out of control. I feel hot, restless, and beyond my capacity to regain control. It feels unbearable. I want it gone. I want a way out.

A Liturgy for When I Feel Furious

Breathe in—*Jesus . . .*
Breathe out—*You can handle my anger.*

I breathe.

God, my soul is desperate for care.
I feel furious.

I feel rage.
The intensity of my feelings scares me.
I feel it in my body.

I won't bully my anger or be bullied by it.
Instead, I open my heart to You, God, in it.

I open, open, open.

My rage must go somewhere.
I release my rage to the only place that can receive it.
Rage blasted on the perpetrator of my pain or toward myself can never redeem my pain.
The only place that can hold my fury is the cross.

Jesus, You received punishment that You didn't deserve.
You took all the blame.
You take the pain of all that is wrong in the world.
At the cross, O Lord, You absorb my rage and return to me . . . love.

God, I know that the tighter I hold on to my rage the tighter it will hold on to me. The only way for my soul, body, and mind to know freedom is to move toward the cross. I bring all my pain, out-of-control anger, belligerent rants, and all my wrath here to You.
I am desperate for my pain to go away.
I am desperate for something to change.
The way out of my rage is the way of the cross because here, I am not alone.

At the end of my guttural scream may the silence afterward offer me the most holy gift of all—freedom.

Anger, released in righteous, powerful love, is the avenue through which God's soft love can be received.

Here, You understand.
Here, You can relate.
Here, You welcome me.
Here, You give me air to breathe.

Here, my anger doesn't destroy, but is redeemed.
Here, I can scream but whisper a cry for relief too.

You are my refuge and peace.
You are my only hope.
You, Jesus, are the way.

You are the only One who can hold my pain.
No amount of my anger can undo what You did on the cross.

When there was violence on the cross—You took it.
When there was mockery, insults, and stone throwing on the cross—You received it.
When there was whipping, mistreatment, and nails hammered into Your hands—You endured.

You take me too.

I give You my fury.
In return for my rage, You make a way to love me.
In return, You bless me.
In return, You promise that resurrection will come.

Even here, Your grace infiltrates my feelings. Even here, You meet me. Even here, You love me.

Living Word

May Your words calm my soul.

> ***Ephesians 2:3–5***
> We all once lived in the passions of our flesh, carrying out the desires of the body and the mind, and were by nature children of wrath, like the rest of mankind. But God, being rich in mercy, because of the great love with which he loved us, even when we were dead in our trespasses, made us alive together with Christ—by grace you have been saved.

lazy

not wanting to attend to the life you've been given

The Language for Feeling Lazy

A big pile of bills mounts on the counter. The sealed envelopes seem to snicker at me. I feel shame. I pass it by again and think, *Not now*. I am so tired. I'm doing many things. These things are good, but they aren't what I *should* be doing. I putter, I fix, I attend, I watch, I disengage, I do. But all the things I am putting my hands on and heart toward are distractions. They keep my mind off the responsibilities I have been given but don't want to do, like facing the reality of my scary financial situation. I do just enough to avoid consequences or the wrath, disappointment, and shame of others. I procrastinate. I am avoiding my life by doing all kinds of things. But really, I am avoiding . . . me.

I am tempted to consume food, pleasure, people, or entertainment. I have an active imagination. I have big ideas, and plans are a form of fantasy. I try to stay busy. I am active, but those actions aren't moving me toward the things that nourish my soul. Rather, they keep me from that nourishment. I want to avoid my pain and anger.

I know slothfulness is a disordered condition of my soul. I am angry. Instead of lashing out in my anger or turning it against myself, I push my anger away. I am angry that my life isn't going the way I want it to go. Instead of facing and accepting responsibilities, I run from them. I am not doing the things I need to do. I can do a lot or do a little, but ultimately, I am avoiding my heart and I disconnect. I become lazy. My actions are causing others pain. No matter how good my life is, I am still not content. I don't want to miss my life by disconnecting from it. As much as I want to do nothing, I don't want to lose my life to laziness either.

For a moment, I let my feelings stay. I feel heavy and lethargic even after I've rested. My mind can't process things clearly. My energy is depleted by small tasks. I just don't want to do the things that need to be done because they stir my deep frustration. I feel a slow-growing dread inside of me.

A Liturgy for When I Feel Lazy

Breathe in—*Jesus . . .*
Breathe out—*I want to be present to my life.*

God, search my heart.

I feel lazy.

I feel it in my body.

Soul, what am I really avoiding?

God, the thing I am avoiding is the very place You intend to love me.

I am afraid of facing what I really feel.

You, God, invite me to enter the places that are hard to see.
You want me to see my disappointment, regret, and sin.
You want me to see my failures.

I don't want to live in a fantasy.
I don't want to blame others or be swallowed up in self-pity.
I don't want to reject my pain, check out, or be ungrateful.

Help me accept the life You have given me.
For all that my life is and all that my life isn't, it is a gift.
Forgive me for the ways I have not attended to it well.

God, I experience the tension of my lack, weakness, and shortcomings. I am frustrated that I am somewhere I don't want to be. With You, God, my anger is safe. With You I can pour out my complaints and cravings.

God, I return to the diligent care You have over my soul.
Even in my aggravation, You love me.
You don't cast me out or look away.
You aren't ashamed of me.
You make a way for me to move forward.

Despite the ways I have fallen short, You are committed to developing my slothful heart into a devoted heart.

By attending to my anger, I am not only coming back to my life, but to my passions.

Even if it is hard, boring, frustrating, disinteresting, scary, or dreadful —I will remain faithful to the responsibilities You have entrusted to me.

Guide me by Your grace to move from a lazy life to a connected life.

Thanks be to God.

Living Word

I will listen to You even if it is hard to hear.

> ***2 Thessalonians 3:11–12***
> For we hear that some among you walk in idleness, not busy at work, but busybodies. Now such persons we command and encourage in the Lord Jesus Christ to do their work quietly and to earn their own living.

jealous

wanting what other people have

The Language for Feeling Jealous

I see her. I am immediately triggered. I want what she has. I want her looks, life, influence, experience. I hate feeling this way. I can't seem to escape my feelings of envy. It feels like poison in my bloodstream. It makes me sick. She makes me feel angry. Everywhere I go, I see her. I see her in my memory, in my mind, in front of me. It isn't fair. Why can't anyone else see what I see? Like a game that no one else is playing, I hold myself up next to her and compete. This feeling is eating me up inside. I feel jealous.

When jealousy consumes me, I am tempted to justify myself. I try to prove to myself that I am right and I should feel this way. I try to manage my frustration. If I can distract myself, I might be able to get away from it. But so often I fall into gossip or slip out hurtful comments to try to get some sort of reaction. I want validation. I become a victim of my feelings. Instead of fighting my feelings, I feed them. I live in a fantasy driven by power. I have been so angry. For so long I have believed that love is a limited resource, a zero-sum game. The more others get, the less there is available for me. If I wanted love, I had to get it. My heart has a disordered understanding of how love actually works. Feeding my jealousy is rotting my soul.

I let my feelings stay for a moment. Memories and images flood my mind. Painful past experiences press up against me. I am so embarrassed by my jealousy. I don't want anyone to know how deeply I harbor these feelings. My feelings are telling me something. It is a painful reality. I am deeply dissatisfied with my own life.

I don't want to live like this, but I don't know what else to do.

A Liturgy for When I Feel Jealous

Breathe in—*Jesus . . .*
Breathe out—*forgive me.*

I feel jealous.

I feel it in my body, and it rots my bones.

God, I open my heart to You.

Expose my heart.

Though it is painful, my heart lies pried open before You.

I am wanting something that You have not given me, O God.

I am seeking affection and attention.

I am chasing admiration and attraction.

I am pursuing, desiring, and craving something or someone that is not mine.

In the absence of this object, I am left with an ache that gnaws at my heart.

Day and night, it gnaws at me.

My mind can't seem to find an escape. My heart races. My spirit is wrestling. I can't think straight.

I feel my jealousy now, but I have known it before. It has pierced me like a thorn throughout my life.

Reveal to me the root of my pain.

In what ways was I not loved the way I needed to be loved?

By my mother or father, God, how was I not seen, heard, or attended to?

The love I didn't receive motivates me to grab for it from other people and places.

I don't want to do this anymore.

I don't want to live trying to get more and more love from something or someone that can never fill the hole I have.

Father, forgive me for the envy I have harbored in my heart.

Forgive me for using others or things to resolve the pain I have.

With You, I am made clean.

Reveal to me my heart.

God, I want another way.

Would Your Spirit redeem my heart?
Spirit, heal my wound. I want to be whole. I don't want to grasp or grab for a life that is not mine.
Spirit, may Your love funnel into the lonely places in my story and bring restoration.

Remind me of Your ever-loving presence with me in the days and nights when my heart went unseen, unnoticed, and uncared for.

My life is a gift.

You saw me then and You see me now.
My life isn't always how I imagined it.
It doesn't always seem fair, but it is mine.
I breathe this air.
I have this body.
I am alive.
I share space with people who sharpen my need for You.

I feel exposed.

Yet even here, Your love is patient with me.
Your love is kind.
Your love is gracious.
Your love is gentle and leading me.

Lord, hear my prayer and my plea for help.

Even as my jealousy is exposed, I am also touched by Your grace. Yes, Lord, this is the place Your love greets me, pulls me in, and attends to me.

Envy feels off the path of goodness, but You have led me here to see the truth of my heart, that I may be made new, made whole, and made free.

Even when I want immediate change, I accept the slow growth You are causing in me.

This place I find myself is evidence of Your love for me.

For this, I give You thanks.

Living Word

I will listen to Your words of love.

> ***1 Corinthians 13:4–7***
> Love is patient and kind; love does not envy or boast; it is not arrogant or rude. It does not insist on its own way; it is not irritable or resentful; it does not rejoice at wrongdoing, but rejoices with the truth. Love bears all things, believes all things, hopes all things, endures all things.

annoyed

irritated by the needs and actions of others

The Language for Feeling Annoyed

I had one thing I needed to get done. One phone call. It wouldn't take long. But I would need to be focused. I would need quiet. I would need a little bit of space so I could think clearly. I just needed a minute, but I couldn't even get that. I can't get anything done. I feel so annoyed. In my annoyance, I lash out. I react quickly. I want to rant or put others down as a way to reclaim my rights. In my irritation, I want to gather more reasons to be irritated.

I am tempted to dismiss my annoyance by setting it aside—*I shouldn't be bothered. It's always my fault. What's wrong with me for feeling this way again?* I beat myself up for not being who I want to be. My anger feels outside of my control.

I don't like feeling this way. I don't even know when it started, but anger grows in me. I feel irritated and on edge. My jaw clenches. I hold on to my annoyance to justify my actions. I wonder if there is a way through my anger that won't bring harm but healing.

What is it that I really want?

What is it that I really need?

A Liturgy for When I Feel Annoyed

Breathe in—*Jesus, help me . . .*
Breathe out—*reclaim my peace.*

I feel annoyed.

I let myself feel what I feel.

I feel it in my body.

Search my heart, O God.

Reveal to me when in my story I have felt this way before.

My heart is on edge. I feel snappy and irritated. Bring cool to my temper.

I notice the way my mind reacts to my frustration. I can confront, run away, and suppress my anger.

For this moment, help me follow my feelings of annoyance. Help me remain close to You as I do.

Instead of trying to fix, You invite me to feel.

You invite me to open my heart to You and pray.
Right in the middle of my irritation, You are here.
As I pour out my agitation, You are here.

You listen and refrain from fixing me because You want to hear more.
You listen to the things that are bothering me.
You listen slowly and carefully to my deeper pain.

God, slow my heart down.

What is *really* bothering me?

Help me see my true pain.
Looking inward can feel complicated and overwhelming.
Annoyance is easier to feel than the real angst that has brought me here.

I have a deep unsettledness within me.

Perhaps I have a dissatisfaction with my life. Perhaps I have unprocessed anger and resentment festering within me from my past. Perhaps I need to feel what resides in the hidden caves of my heart.

Lord, bring out into the open what You would have me know about myself.

Allow me to see where the pain resides. I want something that I can't get. I want freedom, love, connection, control, space, intimacy, peace. I feel powerless to change the reality of my life or change others so that I can get what I so deeply desire.
This is where my anger is really born.

God, You are taking Your time with me. You are aware of my dissatisfaction. You know my desperation for another way, an easier way. I grow impatient for change, but You invite me to slow down. You invite me to be gentle, kind, and curious with my own heart. You invite me to see myself honestly and to entrust my life to Your good will.

God, Help me be patient.
Help me be patient with the process.
Help me be patient with others.
Help me be patient with myself.
I want to receive the life You have given me with grace, hope, and love.

I come into Your slowness, compassion, and care for my life, God.

Shape my heart, in love, to grow in patience.

I give You thanks for this moment because through my feelings of annoyance, You are carving out a way for my pain to come into communion with You.

I will, again and again, return to You.

I will worship You even in this place of discomfort.

I will turn my face to You. In You, there is calm.

Living Word

I wait on You.

> ***James 1:19***
> Know this, my beloved brothers: let every person be quick to hear, slow to speak, slow to anger.

failure

the feeling of not being who you want to be

The Language for Feeling like a Failure

I messed up. I missed my daughter's school performance. She got in the car and wept. It was her moment to shine, and I missed it entirely. I can't ever get it back. I can't erase this memory from her mind that her mom didn't show up when all the other moms did.

I feel as though I have let myself and others down. I wonder if I'll ever get things right. I fear that I won't. Who I want to be and who I actually am are at odds with each other. Guilt weighs heavy on me. Every area of my life is tainted with mistakes—motherhood, marriage, friendships, vocation, health, beauty, body. I hate that I can't be the kind of person I want to be. Even with all my effort, I still fall short. My home needs to be kept up. Relationships need tending. Schedules need my attention. My reputation must be maintained. I can't disappoint people. I can't let anyone down. I strive. I hurry. I am always aware of what I have left to finish. I feel like a failure.

I am tempted to manage my feelings by trying harder. I power through. I feel the pressure to do more, try more, strive more. Even though it is hard, I listen to the pressure and respond by pressing harder. I am also tempted to respond by turning inward. I become self-critical and I turn my anger against myself: *What's wrong with me? I should be better by now. No one understands. It's my fault. I am responsible for everything.* I feel powerless. My soul is left fragile, exhausted, torn up, and bothered. This is where I am.

For a moment, I let my feelings of failure stay. It is uncomfortable to feel these feelings. I am afraid to feel the depth of my failure. It is so much easier to hide from it or hurry through it. I clench up; it's hard to breathe. I'm not sure what else to do.

A Liturgy for When I Feel like a Failure

Breathe in—*My Lord God . . .*
Breathe out—*hear my prayer.*

I feel like a failure.

For a moment, I set aside strong voices that try to dictate my feelings.

Instead, I open my heart to You.

God, my soul needs care right now.
In my fragile state, I may be tempted to turn to anything else but You.
I may be tempted to defend or attack myself.
But I know Your presence with me is my greatest form of protection.

God, for so long, I have believed I couldn't be loved in my failures.
My story is scripted by the pressure to succeed, the desire to conceal weaknesses, and the need to be strong.

You were with me when I wasn't fully loved in my brokenness.

You saw that when weaknesses were exposed, I received wrath, shame, or guilt from those who were meant to care for me.
You know I had to be strong so that I could feel safe.

I want love.
I have sought unconditional love by putting conditions on how to get it. But the kind of love I really want can't be acquired.
It can only come through accepting my limitations.

God, You welcome my weaknesses, but my weaknesses are extremely prickly for me to feel.
I wrestle with releasing the expectations I have for myself and my need for control.
God, I want to be God.

Yet, invite me into a new story.
A story where my feelings of failure aren't to be tucked away but exposed by Your light of love.

You gently call my weaknesses to come out.
You funnel grace, compassion, delight, and love into my fragility.

Help me greet weaknesses, befriend them, and allow them to stay. I feel my failures sting me, prick me, bother me, and annoy me. But before I reach for self-correction or condemnation, I open my heart to You. Your faithfulness meets me in my failures and ushers in the freedom my soul so deeply yearns for.

As I embrace my limitations, I am embraced by Your grace. A grace that loves me despite everything I lack. Your grace sings over me, "My grace is sufficient for you, for my power is made perfect in weakness" (2 Corinthians 12:9).

You have not allowed me to fail as a way to punish me. You have given me a no in my life not as a prison, but as a place to discover Your presence. Accepting this no is an invitation to Your grace for the story You have given me, God.

Here, as Your grace greets me, I can give You thanks.

Living Word

Lord, I am listening.

> ***2 Corinthians 12:8–10***
> Three times I pleaded with the Lord about this, that it should leave me. But he said to me, "My grace is sufficient for you, for my power is made perfect in weakness." Therefore I will boast all the more gladly of my weaknesses, so that the power of Christ may rest upon me. For the sake of Christ, then, I am content with weaknesses, insults, hardships, persecutions, and calamities. For when I am weak, then I am strong.

exhausted

deep tiredness that fuels anger

The Language for Feeling Exhausted

I walked in the house after a long day and looked around. It was a disaster. Trash on the floor, dirty bowls on the table, art projects from last night still on the counter. No one else is aware of the chaos. Even as the kids giggle over a funny video, I can't engage in their joy because everything inside of me is on fire. I throw my bag down and fumes rage up inside of me. I feel so exhausted that it makes me mad.

I just keep pushing. Frustration permeates all I say and do. My anger is my comfort. My exhaustion overtakes me. I say and do things I regret. I hate this about myself. I hate it. Sometimes I use my exhaustion as an excuse to be lazy. Resentment, bitterness, and a quiet anger boil inside of me. I am afraid that there is no end in sight. I am afraid that life will always be this way. Sometimes I imagine giving up, leaving, and walking away from it all.

For a moment, I let my exhaustion stay. I don't fight, resist it, or react to it. Instead, I listen to it. I slow down and breathe. I pay attention to my body. I hear my fatigue, heaviness, and this tiredness that I can't seem to shake. I feel a tightness deep in my bones, back, and chest. Even when I sleep, I don't feel rested.

I try and try and try, but nothing I do seems to relieve me of my exhaustion. I find little reprieve. Even when I act out in anger, it only makes it worse. I don't want to attack or withdraw. I don't want to miss out on a good life. I don't want to live like this.

A Liturgy for When I Feel Exhausted

Breathe in—*Jesus, good shepherd . . .*
Breathe out—*may I find my rest in You.*

I feel exhausted.

I feel it in my body.

I open my heart to You, God.

Reveal to me when in my story I have felt this way before.

God, I am not here by accident.
I am not here by my own misfortune.
I am here because, in Your will, You have allowed it.

I accept that I am powerless to save myself from my circumstances.

I also accept that I am not without power.
For my power, my strength, and my hope come from You.
I return to You now for help.

I've been so overwhelmed that it has brought me to a state of exhaustion.
I am nearing a breaking point.
Everything seems to weigh me down, even small tasks.
I've been asked to do things beyond my limits.

I feel like I am holding on to a branch that is about ready to snap.
I have so many burdens on my back.
I have to climb up and out.
I am failing.
I am afraid that things will never change.
Pressure presses down on me from every side.

I don't want to explode.
I don't want to be resentful.
I don't want to displace my anger onto people who don't deserve it.
It is hard not to become bitter, rude, or mean.

God, help me.

God, help me pass through anger and resentment without using them as weapons to gain power.

God, help me turn toward You with the impossible position I am in.

God, help me believe in the *good* of the journey I am on.
The good is for others in my care, the good is for the spreading of the gospel, the good is for the healing of my own pain.

God, help me endure because I can't do it on my own anymore.
I can't carry this cross alone.

It is harder than I imagined.
It is hard to not harbor anger.
It is hard to forgive.
It is hard to let go.
It is hard to relax.
It is hard to surrender.
It is hard to believe that You care about my life more than I do.

As I dangle from this branch, help me see that You are the tree I dangle from.
Your arms endured that lashing, whipping, and slashing of intense suffering.
Your arms fed the five thousand.
Your arms served the disciples.
Your arms became a resting place for those in need of rescue.

You understand exhaustion too.
You took space to be with Your Father when Your soul and body were weary.
May I learn from You how to rest in God's love.

If it would be Your will, please deliver me from this pain because it is so hard to bear. If my circumstances do not change, may Your grace be enough to sustain me. I pray it would be.

One moment at a time.

What You have entrusted to me, I entrust back to You. I give You my life. Even as weary as I am, may my life be an offering to You.

Lord, hear my prayer.

Living Word

I wait. I listen. I believe the words that You speak are true.

2 Corinthians 1:8–10

For we were so utterly burdened beyond our strength that we despaired of life itself. Indeed, we felt that we had received the sentence of death. But that was to make us rely not on ourselves but on God who raises the dead. He delivered us from such a deadly peril, and he will deliver us. On him we have set our hope that he will deliver us again.

betrayed

the result of someone violating your trust

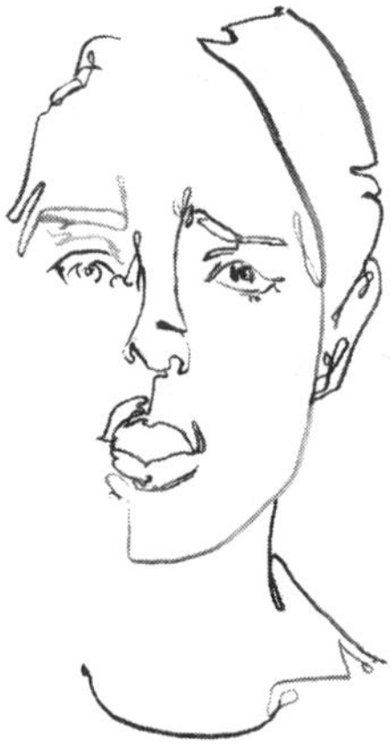

The Language for Feeling Betrayed

You said you needed a break from our friendship. You needed a little space. When I see you now, you give me the cold shoulder and treat me worse than a stranger. How could you do this to me? *How?* That one word confounds me. You get to walk away. You get to live your life as though nothing happened. As though we didn't share something special, you walk away without glancing back. You didn't even check to see if I was okay. Because I'm not. I'll never be okay. I am so mad I ever gave you parts of me. How can I just be an afterthought to you? What we had mattered . . . at least to me. Now I am left with the rubble of what was once beautiful. I am left with the pieces to wedge back together. I am angry that I care as much as I do. I wish I could walk away and wipe my hands of you like you did to me, but I can't. I trusted you. I feel so betrayed.

I want to inflict my pain on you the way pain was inflicted on me. I want you to hurt as much as I do. I want to believe lies as a way to indulge my feelings of betrayal. I want to figure out how this happened and solve it like a mystery. I collapse into my feelings. I believe that because I feel betrayed, I am betrayed.

For a moment, I pause. I just feel. This is hard. Some experience betrayal often. For me, it has only been a handful of times. Each time my soul has been demolished. I let my pain stay. I feel the fire and the grief and the rage. I release the need to make sense of it. This is where I am. I feel my body. My chest is burning. My heart is racing. I listen. My body never lies.

My feelings of betrayal are a signal that my soul is in desperate need of more care. I try to listen with gentleness, curiosity, and courage. I try to remember that God's greatest intention for my life is to love me.

A Liturgy for When I Feel Betrayed

Breathe in—*O God in heaven . . .*
Breathe out—*help me.*

God, here I am.

I feel betrayed.

I am so deeply hurt.

I let myself feel this in my body.

I pay attention to where I have felt this feeling before.

In my feelings of betrayal, I am tempted in many ways.

I resist trying to figure out my feelings in my mind.
I resist finding comfort by nursing my wound with made-up stories.
I resist feasting on my anger.
I resist bringing harm to others or to myself.

God, where, oh where do I find my refuge from such pain?

There is only one place I can go with my pain that will mend my throbbing spirit.

I come to You.

I come to Your table and find communion because You understand my pain. I feast on the bread of life and not my anger.
I drink the wine of Your grace and not the wine of my revenge.
I commune with You instead of collapsing in on my pain in solitude.
I dine in Your company because You understand what betrayal feels like.

You were betrayed by those who promised to protect You.
You were betrayed by the people You fed, served, and provided for.
You were betrayed by those You healed and helped.
You were betrayed by Your closest friends.

Christ, You know betrayal.
You also knew Your Father's love.

I bring my raw, oozing, and angry heart before You, God, my Father.
With You, my heart remains broken, but I don't remain alone.
With You, I believe I will be able to forgive and be free.
With You, I believe this betrayal will not be the end of me, but the beginning of something new.

Though it is painful, I accept that there are things I will never know or understand. I accept that I am powerless to change the past or control the choices of others. God, help me accept the current circumstances of my life with hope, knowing that You will make all things beautiful in Your time.

Help me forgive as I have been forgiven.

Though this pain is excruciating, it is also the place Your love finds me. It is the place where I can make contact with Your love. For this, I give You thanks.

Even when I hurt, my heart will bless Your name.

Living Word

I want to hear from You even when it is hard.

> ***Romans 12:14***
> Bless those who persecute you; bless and do not curse them.

4

happiness

Happy—experiencing joy
Creative—inspired
Safe—feeling secure
Free—unrestrained
Grateful—experiencing thankful acceptance
Peaceful—being at ease relationally with God, yourself, and others
Soft—feeling tenderness
Curious—desiring to explore
Playful—fun-loving
Content—being at peace with your circumstances
Courageous—comfortable with stepping into hard things
Hopeful—anticipating the future
Nostalgic—a tender feeling of homesickness

happy

experiencing joy

The Language for Feeling Happy

I can't hide my anticipation. It spills out the side creases of my closed smile. I glance up at you, nervously eager. You were already looking at me. We make eye contact. We pause and hold our gaze. In a split second, our souls connect. I try not to laugh, which of course, makes me laugh. I can't remember the last time I have been happy. *I'm so happy.* Those words startle me. Savoring this moment, I look outside. Beauty settles deep onto the shelves of my soul. This takes a moment. I feel peace, but something else too. Something in me feels playful and pleased. I know this feeling, though it's vague and nuanced with many other emotions. It's joy.

I am aware that I can use this feeling of happiness as permission to do whatever I want. In my happiness I may be tempted to indulge. I tend to overspend, disregard rules, and take advantage of others. I can let my happiness lead me without considering the consequences. Happiness can also lead me to shame or anxiety. I may feel like I don't deserve the happiness I have, so I don't acknowledge it, talk about it, or allow myself to feel it. I sometimes minimize my joy because I don't want it to cause others who are struggling further pain. I am also afraid that this feeling will flee from me. I want to grab on to it, but I am anxious it will be taken away.

For a moment, I just let myself feel happy. This is good. I try not to overthink it. I let it take up space inside of me. This joy is overflowing out of me. This joy comes from the astounding capacity of humans to do incredible things. Joy is my release. I feel the depth of my joy, and it tickles me. I love it. I am fully delighted. My emotions may splinter into other feelings like anxiety, pressure, guilt. Yes, those feelings are there too, but I don't want to bypass the goodness that God has given me right now. I want to savor it. I want to hold it. The joy I feel is a gift from God. I don't want to miss it.

A Liturgy for When I Feel Happy

Breathe in—*Jesus . . .*
Breathe out—*You are my joy.*

I open my heart to You.

I feel happy.

I feel it in my body.

Joy is found in all that is good, true, and beautiful.
I feel close to You.

God, grant me discernment because I know happiness can deceive me.
Help me be mindful not to monopolize happiness for my own gain.
God, please don't let happiness lead me astray.
I return to Your love over the love of self and others.

Jesus, sometimes when I hoped people would celebrate with me, they didn't.
I felt rejected in my joy.
I was afraid my joy could cause a rift in a relationship.
Sometimes I fear experiencing joy, expressing my joy, or sharing my joy may cause others pain.

God, how have I missed or neglected others in their joy?

This joy is a direct gift from You.
It is out of the abundance of Your love for me.
I still have a hard time believing that I am loved.
I still struggle to comprehend that I am a child in whom You delight.

I am still learning how to receive joy without devouring it or dismissing it.

Jesus, I receive the gift You are giving me now.
Even when I don't believe that I deserve it . . .
Even when I am afraid of losing it . . .
Even when it requires me to be vulnerable—I receive it.

Jesus, I receive this happiness as a form of Your care for me.
Even when I'm tempted to consume it . . .
Even when I don't feel worthy of it . . .
Even if in a moment this feeling will fade away—I let it fill me now.

Jesus, You receive me.

You receive me with tender welcome, delight, and wide-open acceptance.
You receive me with connection, compassion, and assurance.
You receive me with celebration and kindness.
You receive me and I come into Your heavenly wonder.

In You, my joy expands and multiplies.
In this joy, my soul is nurtured in love.
In this place, my body comes into the profound goodness surrounding me.

I don't just know You love me; I feel it.

I hold on to happiness with grace.
I hold on to it with trust.
I hold on to it with slightly open hands, believing that even when this feeling leaves, Your love won't.

As happiness bubbles up—I smile.
As happiness beats my heart alive—I dance.
As happiness stirs my soul—I sing.
As happiness moves my mind to goodness—I clap.
As happiness consumes me—I drink, savor, and dwell in the glory.
As happiness comes over and over again—I celebrate.

As happiness amazes me—I gaze.
As happiness tickles my eyes with the hope of what may come—I give thanks.

Thank You. Thank You. Thank You, God.

God, I worship You.

Creator of life, love, and all things, I come into Your joy.

Here, I am made alive.

Living Word

I am listening to You.

> ***Galatians 5:22–25*** *NIV*
> But the fruit of the Spirit is love, joy, peace, forbearance, kindness, goodness, faithfulness, gentleness and self-control. Against such things there is no law. Those who belong to Christ Jesus have crucified the flesh with its passions and desires. Since we live by the Spirit, let us keep in step with the Spirit.

creative

inspired

The Language for Feeling Creative

For a moment, I see possibilities. I open my laptop. I sit poised with my mind in motion and my heart ablaze. My fingertips slide across the cool keys and a slight smile comes as I lift my eyes to the screen. I plot the story out like tracing a constellation. I open a blank white screen and my fingers type. Words serenade my senses like jazz in a nightclub. The inspiration is rich, boundless, and beautiful. I feel alive. I feel unstoppable. A touch of fear brushes up against me as I nurture all my ideas. *What if I can't do this? What if I fail?* . . . I stare at the screen blaring with rows of black words now. I see hope. I see fear. I see all that I could be. If I look closer and almost through the words, I see me.

I feel creative. I am tempted to create not to commune with God, but to become God. The quiet urge comes to create, make, and strategize a way to get to what I so deeply want. I am tempted to feed these thoughts with grandiose ideas and dreams cloaked in deceptive words like *should* and *have to*. My happiness becomes attached to my accomplishments and the right execution of my ideas. My Tower of Babel is built on my back, brick by brick. A heavy burden.

I am tempted to despair. I shut down, hold under, or set aside my ideas because to hope that anything in my life would or could possibly change is too painful. I shrink back from the possibilities that my creativity opens. I cling, instead, to the ordinary, safe, and status quo.

The truth is that I feel creative. I feel alive and connected to who I am created to be. Energy pulses through my body. I feel close to God here. I feel powerful, strong, and unstoppable. I let these creative feelings stay. I feel excitement and anticipation. I feel my heart race. I feel it come over my thoughts and imagination, and invade even my sleep. I am swept up into the creative process. I wonder where these feelings will take me. I pray they will lead me closer to God.

A Liturgy for When I Feel Creative

Breathe in—*Father God . . .*
Breathe out—*create in me a heart of love.*

I feel creative.

I feel it in my body.

My creativity has a story.

In some ways it has been received, hidden, set aside, or caused me hurt.

But for a moment, I open my heart to You.

God, I feel a spark flickering inside of me.
A small desire is growing.
I feel it.
I can't stop imagining what might come.
When I close my eyes, I see all the pieces falling into place, and my soul accelerates.
I feel something waking up inside of me.
It's risky and right and everything I've been wanting.
I am coming alive.
The anticipation of what could come is all-consuming.
I want to create something beautiful.

God, I believe my hands, heart, and pent-up hope all have a purpose.
I want to pour all of my time, energy, and affection into this new possibility.
The spark wasn't a fire kindled by mere magic.
It came to me.
It was ignited by You.

It started someplace else.
It started in the beginning.

God, You created.

I want to use creativity to get beyond the beginning.
I believe creativity will take me forward, someplace else, somewhere better.
I try to build a structure that will transport me from my reality to a better one in the future.

God,
I resist using these ideas to bring me self-glorification or selfish gain.
I resist using my creativity as a way of escaping reality.

I resist ignoring the creative gifts You have given me because I am afraid of not succeeding.

You know parts of my heart want to manipulate the gifts You've given me in a way that I think will fix or save me.

Create in me a clean heart, O God.

Lord, I willingly, cautiously, and courageously step into this call to create.

I don't have to make something happen, rather I get to move into what You have asked me to do.
I don't have to figure everything out.
I don't have to do anything but be faithful to the task before me.

God, I relax into the wondrous creation of the world, those around me, and my own mysterious soul.
I rest in Your power, God.
You inspire me.
I don't use my power to build beyond You, God,
I use my power to be with You.

God, above all, form in me a creative heart of love.
Let all that my hands do become a doorway to participate and invite others into Your indwelling presence.

Lord, hear my prayer.

Living Word

Lord, I am listening.

> ***Psalm 51:10–12***
> Create in me a clean heart, O God,
>   and renew a right spirit within me.
> Cast me not away from your presence,
>   and take not your Holy Spirit from me.
> Restore to me the joy of your salvation,
>   and uphold me with a willing spirit.

safe

feeling secure

The Language for Feeling Safe

I close my eyes, but I can still see. I can see the willow tree waving with long arms like a broom sweeping the floor. I can see the archway climbing with ivy welcoming me into this secret place. The rock that once stood like a mountain to my little legs now is the place that invites my heart to sit down and be seen. This is my place. I come here when I need a moment to breathe. I come here when my tangled heart needs untying. It's for me. No one knows how this place magically unfolds me and finds me at the same time. Here, I am free. Here, I feel safe.

My soul feels secure. I am aware that I feel other things too. I feel anxious about losing my safety, and I am tempted to trust my safety too much. I must produce a safe environment. I trust in my ability to protect myself. I am in control. I may also be tempted to lose myself to my feelings. I lack vigilance over my own soul. I stop paying attention to what comes and goes into my heart, mind, and body. I let my guard down and forsake wisdom and discernment.

For a moment, I stay. I feel the safety I feel without giving in to the temptations that lure me away from being fully here. Instead, I listen.

I breathe easily. I relax. I feel open. I feel soft. I listen to my thoughts that are calm and clear. I listen to my heart beating at ease. I want to always feel the safety I feel right now. I never want to lose sight of God's love, protection, and provision over my life.

A Liturgy for When I Feel Safe

Breathe in—*Jesus, may I reside . . .*
Breathe out—*within Your care forever.*

God, I open my heart to You.

I feel safe.
I am held.
I pay attention to my feelings of safety.
I am watchful over my own soul like a shepherd over a flock.
I notice everything.
I am vigilant to see where my soul has strayed to or from to find security.

God, I return, again and again, to the safety of Your care.

I am safe because You are safe.

My feelings of safety, now, are a sign that You are with me.
You are bringing me into Your belovedness.
I trust this.

God, I resist finding my safety in another person or in circumstances.
I refuse to depend on my ability to get safety more than I trust in Your ability to give me safety.
I recognize that I am not God and Your ways, though I don't always understand them, are greater than mine.

God, I trust You.

You invite me into Your presence.

You meet me in my secret places.

A home that only You and I know.

I ponder Your goodness.
I burrow into the earth bed of Your heart.
Here is the only place safety can flourish.
In You alone will I abide.
Here, You nudge me to *tell You more*.

I know that abiding requires nothing of me but to stay in Your love.
So I stay here, in Your arms of safety.

I breathe.

Your arms stretched wide on the tree.
No greater safety can be found but in the arms of the One who died to bring me welcome.

God, You are my rock.
God, You are my shield.
God, You are my protection.
God, You are my hiding place.

In You, God, I find my safe home.

Here, my soul sings.

Living Word

I will listen to You.

Psalm 61:1–4
Hear my cry, O God,
  listen to my prayer;
from the end of the earth I call to you
  when my heart is faint.
Lead me to the rock
  that is higher than I,
for you have been my refuge,
  a strong tower against the enemy.

Let me dwell in your tent forever!
  Let me take refuge under the shelter of your wings!

free

unrestrained

The Language for Feeling Free

I put in my two-week notice today at a job that drained me. I was afraid to step down. I didn't want to make my boss upset. I didn't want to displease my coworkers. For years I've been codependent on praise and people pleasing. But today, when I spoke honestly, I felt empowered and weightless instead of enslaved by fear. Speaking the truth breeds freedom, and I feel just that—free.

I am tempted to use my freedom as a ticket to do whatever I want to do or excuse myself from responsibility. I could see my freedom as a sign to pursue my self-seeking desires. Freedom accelerates my desire for power. I am also tempted to put the restraints that once enslaved me back on. In my freedom, I sometimes also feel anxiety and shame. The habit of my heart is to live in fear and not freedom. Fear sometimes feels safer to me. Sometimes I hold on to fear just in case I need it.

For this moment I do feel free. As I breathe, freedom fills my lungs. I close my eyes and listen. My heart swells. My lips smile. The sound of peace within me splits my soul wide open. Here I am, soft and breathing fully. Nothing is tying me down. Nothing is pulling me back. I feel light. My muscles are at ease. My mind is at peace. I breathe effortlessly. I want to savor what I feel now. I feel free because I am free. I am free because God freed me. I hope I never return to the slavery I have been freed from.

A Liturgy for When I Feel Free

Breathe in—*My friend Jesus, . . .*
Breathe out—*I am free.*

God, I open my heart to You.

I feel free.

I feel this freedom in my body.

I will not cling to fear.
I will not listen to lies.
I will not try to prove myself.
I will not avoid my heart.
I will not pretend or demand perfection.
I will not go back to the heavy burden of trying to free myself.

Even as I list the things I will no longer do, I know my desire for safety is strong.
I know how easily I turn to my capacities to garner peace.
I know that I need Your help to learn how to stay free.

God, help me remain in the freedom You have given me.

What does a free person do?
A free person does whatever is in one's heart to do.

You have set my life upon the rock of salvation, and I will be glad.

My heart enjoys, smiles, and savors.
My heart abides, laughs, praises, and plays.
My heart honors, worships, gives, and loves.

Your truth has set me free.
I let my soul experience freedom—I feel it and dwell deeply in it.
In doing so, I remember who I am.
I am beloved, set apart, known, and adored.

God, I will delight in this freedom all the days of my life.
The weight of burden You have lifted makes my heart swell.
This is what I was made for.
This is the way I was created to experience life.

As You created the world, You are creating new life in me.

Because You loved me, I am free.

For this gift, I give You all praise and honor and glory.

Today and forever, amen.

Living Word

This is what You say to me.

> ***Galatians 5:1** NIV*
> It is for freedom that Christ has set us free. Stand firm, then, and do not let yourselves be burdened again by a yoke of slavery.

grateful

experiencing thankful acceptance

The Language for Feeling Grateful

I watch my children play. Gold light lavishly spills through the trees as they dance. Without effort, my mouth parts and these two words slip out: *thank You*. I whisper them, but more than anything, I feel them. I stretch my soul out in such a way that I can savor every second of this joy. Life is not how I imagined it would be, but I find myself so profoundly privileged to be living it at all.

I feel grateful. I confess that with these feelings of gratitude, I also see the temptations of my heart to wander. I am tempted to take all the credit for the things, people, and accomplishments in my life or be anxious that everything I feel grateful for will be taken away.

These temptations lure me away from being present to what I have been given. I tend to cling tighter to people, experiences, and things. I curl in over my feelings. I can easily turn to fear, shame, or self-condemnation. I can even turn my gratitude into a list of *shoulds*. I *should* be more grateful, I *should* do more, I *should* feel more.

But for this moment, I feel what I feel. Peace fills my lungs.

I feel my breath. My heart is happy. My body expresses gratitude in the form of tears. For a moment, thankfulness wells up inside of me.

I allow these feelings to move through me. I can hardly count the goodness in my life. I can hardly contain the joy. For this moment, I feel God. I turn my heart to prayer.

A Liturgy for When I Feel Grateful

Breathe in—*Jesus . . .*
Breathe out—*Thank You.*

God, I present my heart to You.

I feel grateful.

I feel it in my body.

Fear can quietly slither under the door of my thankfulness.
Pride can also reach around me like my own hand patting my back.
I pay attention to the places where my soul bends, twists, and maneuvers away from the purity of my gratitude.

I hold my feelings of gratitude the way I hold something special.
Like holding a baby, I won't be reckless or distracted.
I don't tighten my grip or loosen it too much.
I honor the gifts You have given me, God. "Every good gift and every perfect gift is from above, coming down from the Father of lights, with whom there is no variation or shadow due to change" (James 1:17).

I have been given so much.

I hold every single gift with gentle surrender.
I open my hands.

Thankfulness is on my lips.
With all my heart I give thanks to You, Lord.
I sing my praise, speak my joy, shout my delight.
I let gratitude be the gravity that keeps me grounded in my life.

My thankfulness can exist alongside any feeling.
Anxiety—gratitude.
Sadness—gratitude.
Worry—gratitude.
Confusion—gratitude.

No feeling can cancel my thankfulness, because Your gifts are present in all things.

God, the greatest intention You have for my life is to love me.
And my life, though flawed and fragile, is a gift.
I feel gratitude welling up inside of me.
I will give thanks for it, again, and again, and again.
I will give thanks for my life until my last breath.

For what I have been given, for what has been taken away, for all that my heart holds dear—*thank You.*

Living Word

Lord, I am listening.

> ***Psalm 9:1*** *NIV*
> I will give thanks to you, LORD, with all my heart;
>   I will tell of all your wonderful deeds.

peaceful

being at ease relationally with God, yourself, and others

The Language for Feeling Peaceful

I've been wrestling for a while. My soul has been in turmoil. But this morning at church as the melody strummed my heart I sang through tears, "It is well with my soul." I surrendered. And there it was, peace. I recalled how far I've come. I've lost much, let go of much, been given much, forgiven much, fought much. My soul has made a truce with God, myself, and others. I am free. I am free. I am free.

I feel peaceful. I confess that even this feeling comes attached to whispers of fear. If I listen to the fears, they get louder. I am tempted to lose my peace to the possibility of losing it. I can quickly become the manager of my peace. I must keep peace, get peace, and sustain peace. I notice in my own soul that I am also tempted to forgo my power for the sake of peace. I allow my need for peace to be the driving force of my decisions. I can abandon reason, my agency, discernment, and my desires in order to make everyone else okay. I forsake myself to maintain peace.

I listen to the peace I feel inside of me now. It is good. I pay attention to my body. My body isn't defensive or tight. I'm not clamped down, but calm. I can breathe freely. Peace embodies me.

As my thoughts tempt me away from being right here, with my will I choose to stay with my feelings of peace. Peace is a gift from God.

The Spirit gives me peace that is unattached to my abilities or accomplishments. A quiet calm settles inside of me, and my response is joy.

A Liturgy for When I Feel Peaceful

Breathe in—*Jesus, friend . . .*
Breathe out—*Your peace dwells within me.*

God, I open my heart to You.

I feel peaceful.

I notice how I feel it in my body as I breathe.

Peace fills my heart.
Calmness spreads out within me like a cool shawl to my soul.
I feel free.

Lord, help me discern where my peace comes from.
May it only and always be an outpouring of Your Spirit and not a manipulation of my will to justify what I want.

Soul—dwell in peace.

I dwell in the peace You have given me, God.
I let it take up space like the land does all the way to the sea.
I hold my peace like a mother holds a child.
I cherish my peace like a husband does his wife.
I delight in my peace like an artist does their art.
I give peace to others like a pastor gives out prayers.
Peace. Peace. Peace.
What a gift!
I savor it like water to my dry soul.

Thank you, Lord.
You have reconciled my heart to Yours.
In You there is forgiveness.
In You there is hope.
In You my heart is full.

Love is around me and within me.

You are my great healer.
You are my good Father.
You are my protector.
You are my peacemaker.

Your peace is behind me and before me.
Your peace is now and forever.
I ponder the trinity of peace between You—Father, Son, and Holy Spirit.
You are a God of peace.
I will forever praise You.
Peace fills my soul.
I am well.
I am awake.
I am loved.

Living Word

Lord, I am listening.

John 14:27 *NIV*
Peace I leave with you; my peace I give you. I do not give to you as the world gives. Do not let your hearts be troubled and do not be afraid.

soft

feeling tenderness

The Language for Feeling Soft

I curl my body under the comfort of cotton and cloth. The woven textures cocooning me bring me a warmth I've longed for. I feel a familiar hope drape over my heart, and calmness spreads throughout me. My thoughts move back and forth inside of my mind like a conversation between old friends. I am not undone by the internal banter but experience grace for what is, was, and is yet to come. A gentle tenderness resides within me. I feel free. My soul feels like silk. I breathe ease. I curl my palm around the edge of the blanket and my eyes slowly blink closed. I feel strong. Actually, what I feel is soft. Perhaps they are the same thing.

I confess that with the softness I feel I am tempted to tense up. Softness isn't comfortable for me. I react to my softness by looking for things to tense up about. The eyes of my heart search for danger, especially when I sense there isn't any. I am tempted to deflect away what I feel. I am also aware that I want to settle into my softness so deeply that I can lose my capacity to discern or initiate anything that will disrupt my peace. I neglect my instincts, voice, and wisdom for the sake of continued calm.

For this moment, I allow myself to feel what I feel. I let this softness stay. I feel my body relax. I feel release. I feel safe and accepting. Though I am aware that this feeling is fleeting, I pause to feel. I pause to pray.

A Liturgy for When I Feel Soft

Breathe in—*Jesus, brother and friend . . .*
Breathe out—*may I rest in You.*

God, I open my heart to You.
I feel soft.
I feel this feeling in my body.

I only know softness because I have known hardship.

I know try harder, do more, work diligently.
I know what it is like to feel hurt.
I know the pain of anxiety and anger.

Yet here I am, with a tender heart.
My struggles may not be behind me, but at this moment, I feel soft.
The rough edges of my soul have been made smooth.
God, You have taken my heart of stone and given me a heart of flesh (see Ezekiel 11:19).

Here, I come in contact with Your kindness.
You have exchanged my sin for Your goodness.
My heart of flesh has been molded by Your mercy.
Your tenderness has made me tender.

I let my soul stay soft.

Even as rigid parts of my soul emerge, I resist sanding them down by my strength alone.
Instead, I turn the unfinished places in me to You, God.

God, this softness makes me strong.
It isn't the kind of strength that defeats people, but the kind of strength that doesn't need to.

God, may this softness draw me into deeper dependence on You.
I seek a soft soul, not just for my own sake, but for the sake of others.

O God, thank You.
Draw me ever near.
May I drink from the hope of Your promises.
I set my eyes on You, God.
I gaze upon Your glory.
As I know You, I come to know myself.
As I know myself, I come to know You.
You are soft and You have extended softness to me.
What a wonder to be seen in Your sight as good, clean, and holy.

May this softness be the grace I receive from You and the gift I give the world.

Lord, may it be so.

Living Word

I lean on what You say to me.

Isaiah 54:10
"For the mountains may depart
and the hills be removed,

but my steadfast love shall not depart from you,
and my covenant of peace shall not be removed,"
says the LORD, who has compassion on you.

curious

desiring to explore

The Language for Feeling Curious

For my birthday I was given a trip to Catalina Island. Instantly, joy sparked within me. I hadn't been there since I was a child. I immediately searched the internet for information, feeling curious to learn more about this place. I know this feeling. I know the joy that comes with discovery. I know the anticipation of what could be. I want to know more. Even now, the stirring accelerates because the possibility of something good is within reach.

I enjoy this feeling. I am motivated, delighted, alive. This feeling may easily splinter into other feelings like fear, nervousness, or resistance.

I tend to get lost in this feeling. When I am curious about something, I want to devour it. My curiosity can turn to control. I am tempted to control people or my circumstances. I am tempted to gain knowledge for the sake of control. I can be nosy and intrusive and lack the discernment to honor the boundaries of others.

Curiosity has harmed me before. As curiosity rises in me now, I notice my instinct to shut it down—*don't start a new relationship, don't take a risk, don't try something because it could bring pain, don't dream.* I hush my thoughts.

I am sometimes even tempted to avoid my responsibilities so I can indulge my curiosity. I seek novelty instead of faithfulness.

There is a growing itch inside of me. I feel curiosity in my body. I feel excitement and my heart pacing with anticipation. I feel it in my throat, eager to ask questions. I am so curious to know more, go somewhere, experience something new.

But for this moment, I slow down. In my thirst for more, I don't want to miss Christ. I don't want the object of my affection to replace God.

A Liturgy for When I Feel Curious

Breathe in—*Jesus, brother and friend, help me . . .*
Breathe out—*discover You.*

I open my heart to You.

I feel curious.

God, I love the way You made me.
My heart seeks to know more and more and more.
My hunger to understand and learn and discover is a delight.

In my feelings of curiosity, God, help me be watchful.

I don't want my innocent pursuit of knowledge to bind me in sin.
Help me not to feed a vice in the name of virtue.
Help me, God, to be honest with myself all the way through.

Discovering a new place, person, adventure, thing accelerates my soul.
My dreams, interests, and hopes are illuminated in me as I pursue what is on the outside of me.

I feel like I am coming alive.

As I feel, I am reminded of a youthful place inside of me, a child-like desire to play and delight in surprises.
I was made to feel this kind of joy.
God, You made me this way.

Curiosity wasn't always fostered in me.

Those who raised me didn't always allow me to explore, take risks, and try new things.
Reparent my heart in the way of happiness.
May I be a person who can foster joy in others as well.

God, You are the great curator.
You are the good designer.
You are the great counselor asking questions.

Even though You know everything, You are still curious.
Knowledge isn't Your driving force; love is.
You love to love us.
You love to love me.
You delight in my delight to discover.

You are the great initiator.
You initiated the world.
You initiated humankind.
You initiated healing and hope through Your son, Jesus.
God, You never stop initiating.

As I follow this itch of curiosity, I may discover unsavory places within me, others, or the world.
In such instances, please afford my heart the kindness it needs to see what it is You would have me see.
May my soul remain soft and strong.

My curiosity is an imprint of Christ in me.
May the end of my curiosity always bring me to the arrival of Your love.

Because of this, my heart sings.

Living Word

I am listening.

> ***Philippians 4:8–9***
> Finally, brothers, whatever is true, whatever is honorable, whatever is just, whatever is pure, whatever is lovely, whatever is commendable, if there is any excellence, if there is anything worthy of praise, think about these things. What you have learned and received and heard and seen in me—practice these things, and the God of peace will be with you.

playful

fun-loving

The Language for Feeling Playful

In a rush of childlikeness, I toss my bag into the shopping cart. The warmth of the day pours down like a sunshine-shower all over me. I am so happy. I jump up on the back of the cart and with one foot I push off the pavement. I careen through the parking lot all the way to my car. I can't help but laugh to myself. I am alive. I feel playful.

I am tempted to shut down this feeling. Playfulness is connected to other memories. I was criticized for being fun-loving or too loud. There wasn't time for play; I had to work before I played. Playing wasn't being responsible. In my playfulness, I can miss other people. I see my happiness as the only end goal. So I can disregard the feelings of others to get the laughs I want. I can act inconsiderately, be overly sarcastic, put others down, or antagonize people as a way to bring myself joy, laughter, or a rise.

As playfulness stirs up within me now, I let it. I am happy. I pay attention to how my body holds my joy. I have a giddy feeling in my heart. I feel delighted. I want to move. I feel light. I feel free.

As these feelings move through me, I feel connected—body, soul, mind. I was created to be whole. I feel connected to my creator. My joy orbits around God's joy.

A Liturgy for When I Feel Playful

Breathe in—*My friend Jesus . . .*
Breathe out—*teach me to play.*

I open my heart to You, God.

I feel playful.

I feel it in my body.

Search my heart, O God.

Reveal to me the story of play in my life.
How was my play nurtured?
How was it denied?
How was I loved in my playfulness?

I may be guilty of using playfulness as a distraction from my pain.
I may have pursued playfulness at the cost of relationship.
I may have used happiness as a form of escape.

God, help me see playfulness as an invitation to become who I was created to be.

Creation plays.
I see it.
The trees bend.
The clouds dance.
Rain splatters.

I am Your creation, O God.
The purpose for my mere existence is to play.

I was created for this.
I am wired to enjoy life.

Help me play, God.
Help me do something simply for the sake of doing it.
Help me not to put play and work at odds with each other.
Work has an end goal, but play *is* the goal.

Play is the goal of every relationship.
The purpose of relationships is to play with as many people as possible.
It isn't a competition.
It isn't to gain or get.
It isn't to dominate or overpower.
It isn't to give or take away.
Help me enjoy others purely for who they are, not where they can get me.

Play is grace.

Thank you, God, that You created humanity to relate through playfulness.
What a beautiful way to live!
I step into play with others.
I toast, dine, and skip.
I laugh with my entire body.
I smile, wink, and engage with long-lasting friends.
I remember, God, that You delight in a playful exchange with me as well.

I am Your joy.

You give me the skies to enjoy like a cinema.
You give me the seas to swim in and the waters to float.
You give me the mountains to summit and soar.
You give me the expansive fields to be free.
You give me the gravel road beneath me to run on.
You give me the canvases to color, the words to write, the conversations to be curated.
You give me the melodies to sing and my body to move.
You give me the relationships to relish in.

You invite me into a life of play.

All of life is a playground.

My, God, You are so good.

I give You thanks.

Living Word

I incline my heart to hear from You.

> ***Ecclesiastes 8:15***
> And I commend joy, for man has nothing better under the sun but to eat and drink and be joyful, for this will go with him in his toil through the days of his life that God has given him under the sun.

content

being at peace with my circumstances

The Language for Feeling Content

My teacup is warm between my palms. I sit in the quiet aftermath of a morning filled with hurry. The house is undone and disheveled with shoes, bags, and kids' stuff everywhere. Instead of being bothered, I feel something different. It wasn't sudden, but a slow change like when spring turns to summer. Things I once wrestled with have come to pass. Complaints that once riled me up really don't seem to matter to me as much anymore. Worries that once worked me into a cobweb are easy to release. It's not that I don't care or that I am apathetic; it's that I have peace that all will be well. I have accepted that I can't change other people and that some circumstances really are beyond my control. I am not pushing, thriving, or ambitiously trying to change my life. I believe that the life I am living is a good one even when it is hard. I feel content.

I know contentment because I know what it's like to be discontent. I have struggled with my circumstances. My vocation, financial situation, relationships haven't been what I wanted or desired. I have been annoyed, sad, or worried that things would never change. I have harbored bitterness and resentfulness toward others and myself. I have had a hard time believing that my life was good. My circumstances may still be challenging, but I have a deep sense of acceptance. Here I find myself. I am at peace with my circumstances.

Even still, I am tempted to mistake my circumstances for the source of my contentment. I might easily shift to try to control my circumstances so that I can control my contentment. I may even dismiss my feelings of contentment. I may mistake my contentment for complacency.

But I let my feelings stay. My chest is at ease. My mind is centered. I am calm. I turn to God.

A Liturgy for When I Feel Content

Breathe in—*Jesus . . .*
Breathe out—*I stay close to You.*

God, I open my heart to You.

I feel content.

I feel it in my body.

God, You are inviting me to stay connected to You in all things and through all things.
I stay present to my story and the one You are penning in me now.
Through every circumstance I pray I can abide in You.

Like a vine clinging to a branch, I abide in You.
Like a child burrowing into the curve of her mother's side, I abide in You.
Like a bride slipping a band of promises onto the finger of her spouse, I abide in You.

Where else can I go to find such peace for my soul?
My vocation will fail me.
My relationships will fail me.
My body will fail me.
My mind will fail me.
My reputation will fail me.
My strength will fail me.
But You, God, You never fail, for Your faithfulness is new every morning.

You intend good things for my soul.
I will continue to bind myself to You.
I set my feet not on *my* way, but on Yours.
I remain here.

These feelings of contentment rise up in me and also take root down into me.

I breathe into this peace.
I feel it.
I speak it.
I write it.
I sing it.
I delight in it.
I give thanks for it always and forever.

No matter what the circumstances are, You are my stay.
In You I have all that I need.

I remain close to You, my God and my strength.

Thank you for Your grace that sustains me through everything.

I will worship You all the days of my life.

Living Word

I want to hear from You.

> ***Philippians 4:11–13***
> I have learned in whatever situation I am to be content. I know how to be brought low, and I know how to abound. In any and every circumstance, I have learned the secret of facing plenty and hunger, abundance and need. I can do all things through him who strengthens me.

courageous

comfortable with stepping into hard things

The Language for Feeling Courageous

An educator at my child's school has been making decisions that deeply trouble me. I have been silent for a long time, but I couldn't go another day without speaking out. I looked down at my hand and saw it had a slight tremor. I instantly held it steady with my other one. I knew I was upset, but I didn't realize how upset I was. I knew what I needed to say. But once those words were out in the air, I wouldn't be able to take them back. Words come with consequences. I have something to lose here. I could lose my reputation, my role, my appearance of sanity. But looking away isn't an option anymore. I am afraid. I try to see the other side of this conversation. I look to what could come. *What if the outcome could be good?* When I think of what could be, my courage grows. I let my imagination bypass the possible pain, ridicule, embarrassment, and loss and remember the end goal. I remember my deepest need and value. I want to do what is right no matter what it might cost me. I feel courageous.

I confess that in my big emotions I move to action before I think to attend to prayer. As danger encroaches, I am tempted to lash out. I feel like Peter did when he cut off the ear of the soldier out of reckless courage (John 18:10). I am tempted to abandon courage. Instead of stepping into courage, I respond by crumbling under my lack of it. I lose my sense of agency and power. I feel crushed and defeated. I resist facing what is dangerous or threatening.

For a moment, I let my feelings stay. I attend to my heart. I feel my courage sitting right beside my fear. I feel it in my body.

I pay attention to my thoughts and where they take me. I want to be with God here. God goes with me. Into war, into battle, into famine, into suffering, into grief, into hard things, and into death—I do not go alone.

A Liturgy for When I Feel Courageous

Breathe in—*Jesus, Father and friend . . .*
Breathe out—*I lean on You.*

God, I open my soul to You.

I feel courageous.

Search my heart. Reveal how courage has impacted my story.

Have I been one to step into courage or away from it?

Supply me, God, with courage and more of it.
I need the strength of heart to continue on despite my fear.
My fear can be a great convincer.
It can convince me that the only way forward is to use my power to get what I need.
Fear can also convince me to give all of my power away.

Both of those options—control or lack of it—keep me from being near You.
But You give me courage as an invitation to draw nearer to You.
Courage comes from leaning on You for understanding, peace, clarity, and wisdom.

So I lean on You.
I lean on You when I feel dizzy.

I lean on You when I feel weak.
I lean on You when I want to run away.
I lean on You when I want to hurt or harm.
I lean on You because, in the end, You are all I have left.

Christ, You are my center.
You strengthen the spine of my soul.
Your courage is my courage.

When all the words have been spoken . . .
When I lay my head to sleep . . .
When I come to the end of my life . . .
I want to know that I lived my life with conviction.
I want to know I have trusted You.
I want to know I walked with courage.

I will walk forward bravely, in love, knowing no harm can be done that will undo Your work on the cross.

In my joy, let there be courage.
In my fear, let there be courage.
In my pain, let there be courage.
In my hope, let there be courage.
In my sacrifice, let there be courage.
In my seeking and receiving of forgiveness, let there be courage.

In every conflict that is before me, may I take up the cross and find the strength that I need.

May I humbly kneel at the crossroad of life and death, with the courage to believe that life will always prevail even if it is cloaked in every way with the scent of death.

Lord, thank You for the courage You have given to me to face my fear.

Help me show up, listen to my heart, speak the truth in love, and walk away.

Thank You that when I am weak, You are strong.

Living Word

I tune my heart to listen to You.

> ***Joshua 1:9***
> Have I not commanded you? Be strong and courageous. Do not be frightened, and do not be dismayed, for the LORD your God is with you wherever you go.

hopeful

anticipating the future

The Language for Feeling Hopeful

Every day has been a battle. Well, every day for years has been a battle. My child struggles with anxiety. Going into new situations is stressful. Going into old places can be paralyzing. There have been tears, arms and legs wrapped around me, and screams. But today, he went into his classroom with a wave and a smile. Something flushed through me. Relief. After all this time of waiting, finally, I feel hopeful. I feel possibility. I feel anticipation. My heart swells. Joy bursts out of me. I am fully present.

I am tempted to hold on to hope as a source of strength or believe that I am solely responsible for my future. I sometimes cling to false hope. I can also swing the other way with hope. I suppress my desires and wants. I focus on all the bad things that could happen or what obstacles could interfere with the good that the future holds. My hope splinters into an array of fears.

But for this moment I feel hopeful. I let this feeling stay. I let my imagination explore the possibilities ahead of me without getting too attached. I won't conjure up false hope or entertain my fears. Instead, I let hope be what it is, a feeling. I allow my hopeful feelings to flutter inside of me. I feel it in my body. I feel it in my heart beating with excitement, the light pace in my steps, the ease of my mind to think freely. Hope fills my body and soul. I open up to God in prayer with my hope.

A Liturgy for When I Feel Hopeful

Breathe in—*Jesus . . .*
Breathe out—*my hope is in You.*

God, I open my heart to You.

I feel hopeful.

I feel it in my body.

I hold my hope with vulnerable tenderness.
I resist clamping down on hope.
I resist trying to control it.
I resist managing it, minimizing it, or making it more than it is.
Instead, I simply receive the hope available to me in Christ.

I remember, God, that every feeling is an invitation to discernment.
Help me place my hope in You always.
You are my hope and my salvation.
I place all of my longings under Your care.
I attend to my desires, and I also hand them to You, O Lord my God.
I hold on to You, God, more than I hold on to what I hope to be fulfilled in my lifetime.

More than wealth, more than health, more than dreams, more than success, more than stability, more than anything—I put my hope in You.

I lift my eyes up to the heavens.
What greater hope is there than You?

With You, my hope has no end.
Here, my heart comes into contact with Your love for me.
You are the great giver of hope.

Because of Your great love, I will love You with every breath I have been given.

May all that I am be an offering of love to You.
May my love, delight, and joy bless Your name.
May my hope forever remain in You.

Thank You for the gift of hope.
Thank You for the possibility of brighter days.
Thank You for a way through what has been challenging.
Thank You for meeting my needs.
Thank You for Your sustaining grace.

I consider Your kindness to me.
I ponder all of Your wonderous ways.
I reflect upon the joy You have given me.
Even in all that remains unknown, I will hope in You.

Your hope fills me.
I receive it now with joy.

Living Word

Lord, Your words are true. I will listen to You.

> ***Romans 15:13***
> May the God of hope fill you with all joy and peace in believing, so that by the power of the Holy Spirit you may abound in hope.

nostalgic

a tender feeling of homesickness

The Language of Feeling Nostalgic

I slowly open the door. A familiar fragrance brushes over me. The strange combination of spice and sweat can only be found here. I haven't been here for a while. Maybe a part of me wanted to stay away. I knew being here would bring back tender memories. Tenderness, though good, can also be a place where I bruise easily. I step inside my old home. I feel completely overwhelmed by my senses gathering data like a computer: click, click, click. I hear the laughter. I hear distant music coming from my father's study. I hear my mother's hands hard at work while she hums an old hymn over a stove. I see shadows dash by me as though the game of tag never stopped. I exhale and something inside of me soars, while another part of me aches. The joy is deep and the desire to reverse time woos me. I smile slowly and my cheeks pinch into two round balls the size of peaches. I am deliciously happy. Something about being here is good. I feel nostalgic.

I confess I feel drawn toward this feeling and yet want to push it away. I have a deep longing for home. I'm tempted to stop my emotions because the feelings are so tender. This feeling splinters into regret, sadness, and fear too. Because these emotions are so powerful, I try to regain control to protect myself from pain.

I am tempted to follow nostalgia down a never-ending path that keeps me from being present. The warmth of these memories satisfies something so hungry inside of me that I get lost in the past. I want to forsake the present for the ponderings of the past.

I let these feelings stay for a moment. I let memories fill my mind.

My heart is full of fondness for what was. I listen to my body. I stay. I am aware that memories lead me somewhere. Where they lead me, I can't always fully know. But something is enticing me and drawing me back into my story. I turn my attention to Christ.

A Liturgy for When I Feel Nostalgic

Breathe in—*Jesus, brother and friend . . .*
Breathe out—*may I find my home in You.*

God, I open my heart to You.

I feel nostalgic.

I feel it in my body, and I am drawn into the stories You have written in my life.

I am homesick for the life I once lived.

Memories of such a happy time are stirred up.
A time without harm, hurry, or hurt.
I ache for innocence, beauty, and peace.
I long to be careless, free, and cared for.

God, as these feelings surface, they are leading me.
I am led to faces and fragrances.
I am led to sidewalks and summers.
I am led to laughter and loved ones no longer here.
All these feelings entice me to one place—home.

These feelings of nostalgia are an invitation from You to be led back home.
I don't have to control my feelings.
I don't have to let my feelings lock me in the past.
Instead, I allow these feelings of nostalgia to cultivate in me a deeper desire for home.

I let sadness, loss, and longing come beside me as well.
I let memories arise without being the gatekeeper of my pain.
I let what I feel come forth.
I accept the invitation with honor because it is from You.

Though grief and gratitude greet me along the path, You invite me to be loved.

Tender memories satisfy me.

They don't ultimately save me, but they inform me.
I miss a place, a person, a season that was very safe and very good.
Grief is evidence that something or someone mattered to me.
The ache yanks on my heart, but it also comforts me.

God, You know.
You were with me then as You are with me now.
You see the memories I see.

I listen to Your words comfort me:

> "Let not your hearts be troubled. Believe in God; believe also in me. In my Father's house are many rooms. If it were not so, would I have told you that I go to prepare a place for you?"
>
> John 14:1–2

That season of goodness from years before is not over.
It lives in the safest part of my being.
It is kept safe like a locket bound around my neck.
I know the greatness of heaven now because of what I was given in the past.

I feel nostalgic.
I remember the memories.
I enter what was once so good and give thanks because it shaped who I have become.
I let my homesickness be the place I allow hope to find me.

God, You are here.
Longings fill my body as though they were my flesh.
I not only reach for the past, but I remember the profound hope I have for the life that is yet to come.

I believe in You and the promise to welcome me into heaven.
A home without sorrow or tears and a joy that will never fade away.

In these promises, my heart is at peace.

Thank You for what once was.
Thank You for what is.
Thank You for all the goodness yet to come.

Living Word

Lord, I will listen to Your truth.

> ***Ecclesiastes 3:1***
> For everything there is a season, and a time for every matter under heaven.

5

disgust

Disgusted—intensely disapproving something offensive

Awful—experiencing something very negative

Sick—being physically unwell

Indecisive—not knowing what to do

Misunderstood—not being seen for who you are

Dread—not wanting to do something you feel obligated to do in the future

Resistant—not wanting to step into something that isn't the way it should be or the way you want it to be

Icky—not liking who you are or what you did

Embarrassed—self-conscious, ashamed, or awkward

Pressure—the suffocating feeling that comes with carrying the expectations of others.

disgusted

intensely disapproving something offensive

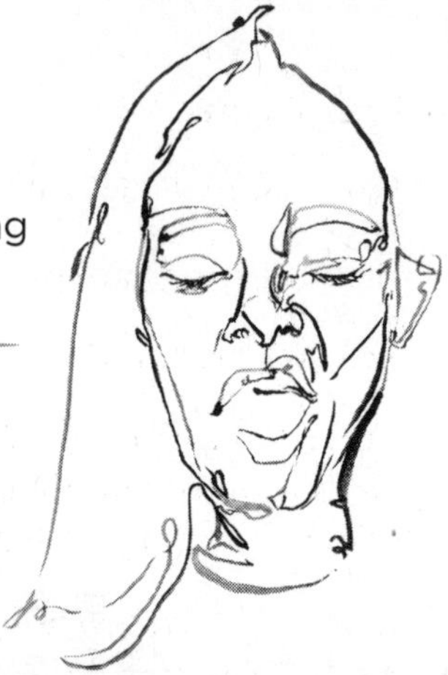

The Language for Feeling Disgusted

The movie was graphic. The story was true. My body feels incredibly uneasy. My stomach hurts. The perverseness in our world is sickening. I can hardly believe what is happening. I can't believe what people are capable of. My soul is bothered by the pain and injustice. A thousand thoughts rush through my mind. I feel disgusted.

I am tempted to get rid of my feelings as quickly as possible. I don't like feeling this way. I want to fix it. I feel anger, irritation, and even loneliness too. Instead of feeling what I feel, I try moving to something else. I shift to blame or self-pity or anything else. Disgust is eating me up on the inside. It gnaws away at me. It consumes me.

My body holds my feelings. My gut reacts, my back tightens, my legs feel weak. My body contains my discomfort.

For a moment, I let myself feel the weight of my feelings. I don't police my feelings or pretend they aren't there. I just feel. My soul needs nourishment. I need understanding, compassion, wisdom, and words. Maybe I don't need to get out of this feeling. I need to be loved in it.

A Liturgy for When I Feel Disgusted

Breathe in—*Father God . . .*
Breathe out—*help me hold on to Your grace.*

I open my heart to You now.

I feel disgust.

I feel it in my body.

God, I was triggered by something, and I am not okay.

Reveal to me how this feeling has been a part of my story.

There is a warning upon my soul.
I have ingested something that is ruining me right now.
I want everything resolved.

God, even here, You invite me into Your presence.
You want all of me to stay close to You.
You are unmoved by circumstances, but You remain a constant presence of steadfast love.

You invite me to be with You in all that is wrong in the world and in me. You invite me to digest my disgust with You.
Help me to let this feeling move through me.
Reveal to me Your love even if a part of me wants to resist it.

Lord, help me accept Your help.
So often, I want to deal with things alone.
I want to vindicate myself.
I want to fix things, others, and myself.
Lord, please help me even if I have a hard time asking for it.

Help me walk the way of willingness.
Help me not to bring harm to others or myself.
Help me.
In my disgust, may I be led to deeper dependence on You.

God, guide me through Your word.

I need Your grace.
We need Your grace.
I can hang my hope on Your undeserved care.
Seal Your grace to my heart, O God.
May it be what frees me.

I ingest Your grace.
I drink it in.
Your grace moves all that is icky out of me.

In my disgust, I believe in Your goodness, Your truth, Your hope, Your love.
I accept it all.
I accept the reality that I don't know what to do.
I accept that I am here with the mess I feel.

Your grace is the medicine that cures my uneasy soul.

Your grace washes out all that is ugly.
Your grace unties all that is tied up inside of me.
Your grace frees me to love.
Your grace helps me begin again.

In You I trust that all that is wrong will be made well.
In this life or the next, Your righteousness will restore all that is ill.
I entrust my life into Your care.

In the most mysterious way, You meet me here.
Even though this feeling is uncomfortable, I am found by You through it.
And for this, I give You thanks.

Living Word

I will listen to You, God.

Psalm 57:1–2

Be merciful to me, O God, be merciful to me,
for in you my soul takes refuge;
in the shadow of your wings I will take refuge,
till the storms of destruction pass by.
I cry out to God Most High,
to God who fulfills his purpose for me.

awful

experiencing something very negative

The Language for Feeling Awful

He walked out the door without looking over his shoulder. His countenance was heavy but restrained. He held back his tears. He wouldn't give me his sadness. I watched him until he drove away. My eyes were searching for his eyes. I wanted contact. I wanted him to assure me with a single glance that all would be well. I needed a glance, a gesture, a nod, anything. But instead, he drove away. He took my heart with him. *What was I left with?* My grief was bound to his grief. I can't live with myself knowing that I hurt someone. I've betrayed him. I have betrayed myself. Now my insides are punishing me. I feel sick for what I've done. I feel awful.

I just want to be done feeling this way. I have to get this feeling out of me. It is eating me alive. I can't eat. I can't escape. So instead of fighting, I give in to my feelings. I lose control. I blame. I self-condemn. I crumble. I believe that I am as awful as I feel. Nothing works.

For a moment, I pause. I slow down my soul. I listen to my body and thoughts. Everything hurts. I let my feelings stay without trying to fight them away or fall prey to their accusations. I just feel awful. I want to be done with this. But more than freedom, I want to be found by God. I don't want a temporary fix; I want true freedom.

A Liturgy for When I Feel Awful

Breathe in—*Jesus . . .*
Breathe out—*help me.*

God, I open my heart to You.

I feel awful.

I feel it in my body.

Reveal to me, God, when I have felt this way before. Perhaps there is grief from my past that has yet to be fully felt.

God, this awful feeling feels impossible to escape.
It's an icky feeling that is sticking to the inside of me.
One negative thing after the last attacks me.

God, help me to stop fixing, working, defending, justifying, or attacking my way out of my pain.
I resist peeling and prying all these complex emotions off me.
As many unpleasant things attach to me, instead of fighting back or falling helpless into my emotions, I ask You, God, for help.
I feel what I feel.
I bring all of me into Your love.

My awful feelings were brought on by my actions or the actions of others.
Maybe even both.
But here I am.

Like the woman caught in adultery (John 8:3–11), I have come to the end of myself.
Guilt, shame, and fear have pounded me.
When it seems like there is no way out but death, You, Jesus, made a way.

You wrote words on the ground.
Words for her.
You wrote in the one place where this woman would be able to receive them. She stood with her head down, body down, eyes down, and You wrote words where she would see them—down.

Below her shame, dread, despair, anger, and exhaustion, You bent down to be with her.

You came down to earth to be with us.
You came down into evil.
You came down into chaos.
You came down into pain.

Your life is a story of coming down.
You bent down to serve.
You bent down to wash.
You bent Your body down to die.

When my countenance is down, You come down beside me and meet me with grace.

I don't have to bear the weight of my negative feelings alone.
I don't have to be buried under them.
Instead, I read the words that You have written for me.

I come close to Your life-giving words.
I look down, not in despair, but in hope that You are writing healing words in my heart even now.

You say, *Wait, you aren't alone, I see you, come, nothing can separate you from my love, I will be with you always, trust not in man but in me.*

Right here, with my spirit downcast, You meet me.

You are near me.

I cling to You.

I need You.

It is by grace alone that You meet me in my awful feelings. For Your kindness to me, I give You praise.

Living Word

I will wait to hear from You.

> ***John 8:3–8***
> The scribes and the Pharisees brought a woman who had been caught in adultery, and placing her in the midst they said to him, "Teacher, this woman has been caught in the act of adultery. Now in the Law, Moses commanded us to stone such women. So what

do you say?" This they said to test him, that they might have some charge to bring against him. Jesus bent down and wrote with his finger on the ground. And as they continued to ask him, he stood up and said to them, "Let him who is without sin among you be the first to throw a stone at her." And once more he bent down and wrote on the ground.

sick

being physically unwell

A Language for Feeling Sick

For days now I have lain here hurting. My body is betraying me. Little I do makes a difference. I hold off fear like a dam. I am too weak to let my mind wander to dangerous places. Fear wraps around me like a snake—slow, sly, and relentless. I try to rest. I try to relax. I try to heal, but I am impatient with the process. I want to be better. I want to return to regular life. I want my normalcy back. I grow resentful of those who can carry on with life. I can hardly think clearly. I so badly want things to change, but I feel powerless. I feel my inability to control anything. I don't like needing help or being a burden. But here I am. I feel so sick.

This pain is an interruption to my life. I try to get through it. I try to get up and back to life before my body is ready. I ignore my body and heart and push through the pain. Quiet thoughts creep in and whisper, *You will never get better.* These dark thoughts weigh heavily on me. In a moment, I am overwhelmed by despair, disappointment, or slow-growing discouragement.

I feel physical pain and emotional pain. Everything in me aches. *What do I do when my body is weak and my heart grows weaker?* I close my eyes and feel the weight of my sickness. My soul is weary. I want out of this, but more than anything, I want to know God hasn't forsaken me.

A Liturgy for When I Feel Sick

Breathe in—*Father God . . .*
Breathe out—*help me be here.*

God, I open my heart to You.

I feel sick.

My body is not well.

Reveal to me the ways sickness has impacted my story.

I want to be out in the world with people I love.
I want my face to feel the warm sun.
I want my hands to touch the crumbling earth.
I want to be anywhere but here, with my body bound to this bed.
I want to move without my body screaming.
I feel like I am being held hostage.

I want to be normal.

I don't want to be here.
I beg You for reprieve.
I plead for You to turn the tide of my pain.

God, help me be where I greatly resist being.
Hear my distress.
Hear my discomfort.
Hear my request for another way.
I have nothing to give.
My words are but a breath.
My body is worn with illness.
I am so tired.

People come and go.
Their presence is a gift.
The kindness of others is a brief balm to my soul.
The faces of good healers help and offer hope.
I drink in this comfort.

I drink in this grace.
But in the end, I am the one left here, alone in my body.

God, I pray, please do not lose sight of me.
In waves, I can feel forgotten, frustrated, grateful, and even sad.
There is a storm of feelings inside of me.
I know by now that I must not let myself be swept out to sea by my emotions.
I must seek to maintain a calm center because feeling all my feelings takes energy that my body needs for rest instead.

Hear my prayer for help.

Help me be patient.
Help me rest.
Help me accept the life You've given me.
Help bring answers.
Help me know that You are trustworthy to hold my pain.

You are the God who made the expansive sky and stars.
You hold everything and everyone within the boundary of Your love.
You bind the sea by the boundary of a single word.
You are the God who binds my pain.
You, Lord, tell the ocean of my pain to stay and not go beyond what I can bear.

Even here, when my body is weak and my heart is frail, I can trust that You, Lord, will not let the waves of my pain go a smidge beyond Your consent. To my pain You say, "You shall not pass."

Let my anger, despair, and discouragement all be evidence of my faith in You, God.

This bed is not a prison, but a place that You have given me to rest into the grace of each breath.
Here, I heal.

I would not choose this way.

The way of weakness can be a lonely walk.
Yet to my surprise, I have discovered a secret that the strong ones do not know.

I know You in a profound and pure way.
I know You in a way that is almost holy.
I know Your voice and You know mine.
I know the gift of every breath.

In the quiet moments, I can even give thanks because in sickness and in health, You are all I have.

My broken body finds communion in Your broken body.
You know sickness and suffering too.
In my body, I am not alone.

Everything is grace.

Living Word

I want to hear what You have to say.

> ***Psalm 73:26***
> My flesh and my heart may fail,
> but God is the strength of my heart and my portion forever.

indecisive

not knowing what to do

The Language for Feeling Indecisive

I sit in the waiting room. My doctors recommend medication. They say it will help me heal, but I worry about the ways it might hurt me. The conversation goes round and round with no resolve. I don't know what to do. My body, mind, and emotions are jammed. I am stalled. I am tempted to work hard to find an answer. I think and rethink. I ponder every possible scenario. But no matter what I do, nothing brings about an answer. I postpone and procrastinate for as long as possible because making a decision is so hard.

I stay with my feelings of indecision without moving toward figuring things out or fleeing. My heart feels tense. I feel exhausted, frustrated, frantic, anxious. For a moment, I don't need to find an answer, but stay with the angst that comes with not having one. I don't know what to do. I keep waiting. I want an answer. I want to know God's will.

A Liturgy for When I Feel Indecisive

Breathe in—*My Lord God . . .*
Breathe out—*help me wait on You.*

I open my heart to You, God.

I feel indecisive.

I feel it in my body.

Reveal to me what is really going on in my heart.

What am I really resistant to?

God, my soul is in distress.

You, God, meet me here in this feeling that is uncomfortable.
In this place of rocky soil, You come beside me.
With You, I try to trust that no matter what choice I make, I will be okay.

As I stay in this waiting place, please give me discernment. As I stay, help me to be honest. As I stay, help me have the courage to face my pain.
Attune my heart to hear Your will and Your way.
Attune my heart to hear my desires and disorders as well.
Attune my heart to listen.

Spirit of God, help me hear.
I don't listen to voices that produce panic in me.
These voices of panic come with a tinge of shame, condemnation, pressure, or guilt.
These are the voices that unknowingly whisper, *You are responsible for the outcome of your life. If you make a mistake, your life will be ruined.*

Your voice sounds different, God.
As I follow Your voice, it feels like stepping on a rock that can sustain my weight.
Even with fear, the ground I walk on will hold me.

So many voices try to inform my soul.
Some hold me and some cause me to slip.
When I step on stones that I must support on my own, I will surely sink.
When I step on stones of faith, I will be afraid, but I won't fall.
God, this is the way of discernment.

God, I trust You with my life.
God, I trust You will not allow this decision to keep me from Your love, grace, forgiveness, provision, hope, and peace.

God, please provide trustworthy people, miracles, words of wisdom, and lights in the darkness that will direct my path.

In time, I trust that stone by stone, You will make a path forward for me. In love, You will help guide me to the answer I know is right, true, hard, but ultimately good.

For this moment, remind me of Your love for me.
You don't rush me or hurry me.
You don't shame me.
My indecision doesn't deter You from me.
You are patient with me.

This place of indecision is the very place where Your love will funnel in.
For Your profound grace that guides me, I give You thanks.

Living Word

Your words are true. I will listen to You, Lord.

Psalm 130:6
My soul waits for the Lord
more than watchmen for the morning,
more than watchmen for the morning.

misunderstood

not being seen for who you are

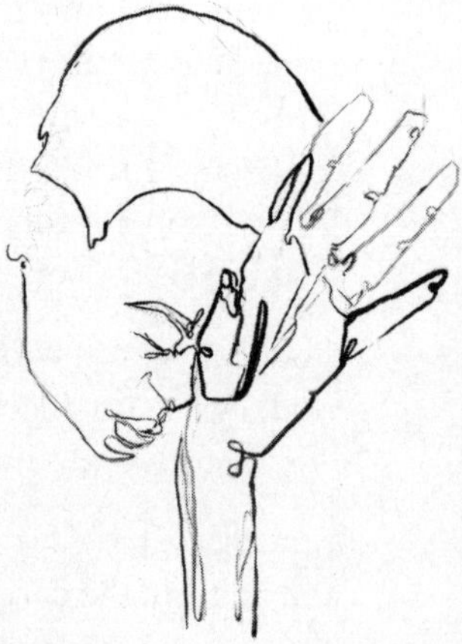

The Language for Feeling Misunderstood

We texted back and forth. I read each text several times. What was she saying? I wrote my return text slowly. I pressed *send*. Then I waited. No response. Several times throughout the next few days I went back to read our awkward exchange. I wanted to take back my words or overexplain what I had written or delete the entire thing altogether. I hate feeling this way. How do I say things in the perfect way so that my intentions will be understood? I hate being put in a box I can't get out of. I hate when someone else writes me off or assumes things that aren't true about me. I feel trapped and every option feels painful and hard.

I react quickly. I react by planning my actions in such a way that no one could ever misunderstand me again. I manage my feelings. I overexplain or analyze the situation from every possible angle. I turn inward with my emotions too. I wrestle with myself. I wrestle with my *shoulds*. I exhaust myself trying to resolve things. I've been here before. I've been on the receiving end of accusations. I feel trapped and vulnerable. The only way out that I see is to live with a wall of protection around me.

For a moment, I let myself feel what I feel without trying to do anything else. I just feel. I feel my body too. My jaw is tense, my stomach twists up, I can't sleep. My thoughts are racing with internal arguments, confusion, anger, and angst. I just want to resolve the situation so I don't have to feel this way anymore. I'll even accept responsibility for wrongs I didn't commit so I can be free from these feelings. But resolving this situation does not actually resolve my pain. My pain from not being seen, known, or fully loved has been there for a long time. There is no simple way out of how I feel. Instead, God invites me to stay with my feelings *with* Him.

A Liturgy for When I Feel Misunderstood

Breathe in—*God, my Father . . .*
Breathe out—*hear my prayer.*

I open my heart to You.

I feel misunderstood.

Search my heart, O God. Reveal to me when in my story I have felt this way before. Is there pain in my past that I have yet to feel?

If so, lead me in the way of healing.

God, I need Your care and compassion.
My feelings of being misunderstood are a signal to me that my soul is snagged somewhere.
I've been misjudged by another person.
It makes me feel terrible inside.
No matter how hard I work, I still feel wronged, judged, and labeled unjustly.

God, I want out of this feeling, but more than instant freedom, I want deep healing.

You, God, know my story.
You know how many times I've longed to be known, but I was missed by people who were meant to pursue me.
I was dismissed, not believed, or played a part to keep the peace.
But all the while, I went unseen.

My feelings now recall the feeling I've felt for so long.
God, I so badly want to be known.
I lob this longing onto the backs of other people.
I give them the weight of my pain to resolve.

I placed too much of my significance on the shoulders of another person. I've needed this or that person to understand me a certain way in order to feel validated.
I've believed that if they understood me, my pain would be gone.

Yet, that is a burden they cannot possibly bear.
The weight is too great.

But I am not alone.
You go with me into the dark depths, O God.
You sow understanding into the deep pockets of my soul.
As I know You, I begin to know myself.
As I know myself, I know You.

Give me courage to face the unknown parts of my own heart.

Help me, God, to be honest.
I am afraid to see parts of myself that I don't want to see.
I am afraid to see the places where I may, in fact, be wrong.
Help me receive others in love no matter how they may perceive me.

God, I give others the right to be wrong about me.
I let go of the need to be seen as fully good in everyone's eyes.
I release my reputation.
I place myself in the judgment seat and take all that comes.

What is my defense?

I am Your child.

I belong to You.

This seat, though false judgments are cast in my direction, is not a seat of execution, but a throne of grace.
This is where You find me.
This is where I find You.
This is where healing happens in me.

For the crevice wound where uncontrollable accusations hurl toward me and my pain is pierced is the same place where Your love pours in.

God, I am forever received and understood by You.

Living Word

Your words are the words of life. I am listening.

> ***1 Corinthians 13:11–12***
> When I was a child, I spoke like a child, I thought like a child, I reasoned like a child. When I became a man, I gave up childish ways. For now we see in a mirror dimly, but then face to face. Now I know in part; then I shall know fully, even as I have been fully known.

dread

not wanting to do something you feel obligated to do in the future

---

The Language for Feeling Dread

I don't want to meet up for coffee. I have postponed this date for as long as I could. I have been putting off this conversation for a long time. It is a hard one to have. We've been friends for so long, but I've been hurt so many times. I can't go on like this. But now that there is a date on the calendar, I want to find a way out. I search my mind for excuses that aren't lies—I am too tired, I have another conflict, I'm overcommitted. All of these are true, *kind of*. I dread what will happen. I am tempted to avoid communicating because I want to avoid this feeling. The weight of trying to break my plans feels almost worse than keeping them. If I go, I'll show up, but leave quickly. I rush through my dread because I don't want to face the hard things. I'll keep my word, but I won't stay long. I'll push through it. The nagging need to just get it over with pesters me. I notice how resentment is creeping in. I am angry that I have to do something I don't want to do. I'm kicking myself for saying yes. The thought of going makes me feel sick. Canceling feels complicated. I don't see a way through this. I feel awful either way.

For a moment, I allow myself to stay with this feeling of dread. My body is oozing with it. I feel it in my back, gut, chest. I resist pushing it away. I let myself feel the weight of it. I notice all the ways I want to fix my problem. If I can just fix the problem, I won't feel this way. But this isn't entirely true. It's a temporary fix. There is a reason I feel dread that is beyond this circumstance. I don't want to feel dread, but more than anything, I want to understand my own soul. I want to know God here.

A Liturgy for When I Feel Dread

Breathe in—*O Lord my God . . .*
Breathe out—*You are with me here.*

God, I open my heart to You.

I feel dread. I feel it in my body.

My feelings of dread are a signal to me that my soul needs care.

I curiously attend to my soul with kindness and courage.

I remember that Your greatest intention for my life is to love me.

God, I've felt dread before.

I don't want to do what is ahead of me.

I have said yes when something inside of me says no.
Somewhere in my story I learned to set aside my desires.
My words weren't congruent with my true desires.

I do believe there are times to say yes when it isn't convenient or a desirable action.
But even on those occasions, You invite me to involve my heart in the process.

Help me now, O God.

My body isn't in alignment with my heart.
Let the words of my mouth be a true reflection of my heart.
Help me believe that I can be loved when I say yes and when I say no.

You invite me to walk in love and be shaped in love.
In this place of dread, O God, You have given me a choice.
The choice isn't to get out of my dread or to be overcome by it, but to be with You in it.

God, I attend to Your love for me in honesty.
I don't want to do this.
I don't want to go.
I don't want to face what is before me.
It takes away more from my soul than I think I have to give.

God, walk with me.
You go with me in kindness.
You go with me and freely love me.
You go with me into death.
You go with me, before me, and remain ever beside me.

May all that I am be a blessing to You.
May my words, actions, and entire life be a living offering of love to You, my God.

God, instead of getting me out of my dread, may Your love meet me in it.

Lord, hear my prayer.

Living Word

You speak the words of life. I want to hear from You.

> ***Ephesians 5:2***
> And walk in love, as Christ loved us and gave himself up for us, a fragrant offering and sacrifice to God.

resistance

not wanting to step into something that isn't the way it should be or the way you want it to be

---

The Language for Feeling Resistance

She asked nicely for help. I picked up the phone to respond yes, even though something inside of me was tensing up. Something inside of me also was saying no. The thing before me is neither entirely good nor entirely bad, but my soul senses a stop sign. I feel resistant. I brushed it off because it doesn't make sense to me. I say, "I'd love to help out!" I felt like I *could* help, so I *should* help. Immediately, my heart sinks. I am overwhelmed. I ignored the warning signs. I am good at avoiding my own heart. I missed myself in this decision. I glided over what I really felt, which was exhaustion. I added more to my plate. It's not that I should say no every time I feel like it; it's that I neglected to engage God and my heart in the process before I answered. Now that I have committed myself to a task that I don't really want to do, I feel a strong resistance.

I am tempted to run away or run through my resistance. But for a moment, I greet my resistance with welcome. Let it stay. I make space for it. I can feel my body tighten up. My chest clamps down as though my body is bracing for something. Something inside of me makes me want to stop. I feel a little bit bothered. I want to understand the gift of this feeling. Perhaps God wants to invite me into His love through it.

A Liturgy for When I Feel Resistance

Breathe in—*Father God . . .*
Breathe out—*help me to dwell in Your love.*

I open my heart to You, God.

I feel resistant.

Allow me to see how resistance has shaped my story.

God, I pause.

You are making space for my tight soul to breathe.
You give me permission to wait.
You have shown me my true desires through my body.
You invite me to rest on the roadside of my resistance and receive care.

My soul has been sprained.
You invite me to slow down and engage my heart with Yours.
You invite me to remember that You care for the places within me that I so easily neglect.

But here, as I move toward stillness, the murky water below my feet starts to become clear.
I can see what is really going on in my soul.
I feel tired.
I feel annoyed.
I feel worried.

As I rest, I hear many things.
I hear my thoughts.
I hear my fear.
I hear my angst and anger.

Help me to also hear Your love.

You give me words that nourish my soul.
You will go with me.
You will give me peace.

You will fight for me.
You will sustain me through any circumstance.

God, help me be wise with the heart you've given me.
Help me listen to her.
Help me be gentle with the whispers she offers me.
Help me lean on Your Word for the nourishment my soul needs.

Help me not to fear my resistance, but to receive it and grow from it.

May I be curious about my feelings and find kindness for myself in the process.

For resistance becomes the next rung on the ladder leading me closer to You.

I receive this resistance as a gift because it draws me nearer to You.

May the resistance I feel be the door leading me into Your dwelling place of love.

You are with me when I stop.
You are with me in this challenging situation.
You will be with me on the other side of it.

Thank You that even here, Your love greets me with grace.

Living Word

God, I am listening.

> ***Ephesians 5:15*** *NIV*
> Be very careful, then, how you live—not as unwise but as wise.

icky

not liking who you are or what you did

The Language for Feeling Icky

My imagination has become my enemy. I've let my mind go off into distant places, and I don't know how to come back. I let my walls down and explored enticing yet dangerous scenarios. And now I feel icky inside. I almost feel sick. I can't get this feeling out of me. I want to scrape it off. But like honey it sticks to me. It's attached to me. I feel gross. I don't want others to be near me. I don't want to be near me either. I can't seem to escape it. What I did plagues me. It almost haunts me. I am tempted to get rid of this feeling by thinking my way out of it. I plan ways to get the gunk on the inside of me out. I stay busy. When that doesn't work, I blame others for the circumstance I am in. I take too much responsibility or not enough. I avoid my heart. I grow weary of fighting my feelings, so I fall into them. I drown in them. I can't find a way out, so I sink into my shame and false narratives. I give way to self-condemnation. Nothing I do seems to make a difference. I can't imagine ever being clean inside. I feel stuck. I don't want to go in. I don't know how to get out.

I let my ickiness stay. I can't shake myself free of it. I feel jittery, uncomfortable, and bothered. I accept that condition of my soul right now. I accept that I am powerless to clean myself up. I am powerless to break free. I am powerless to control how my heart is responding. May the promise of God's love be the substance that sets me free.

A Liturgy for When I Feel Icky

Breathe in—*Jesus* . . .
Breathe out—*purify me*.

I feel icky.

I feel it in my body.

God, I open my heart to You.

I want a way out.
I struggle with who I am.
I wish I were different.
I feel disgusted by the things I've done, the things I've said, and the thoughts I have.
I can't get clean on the inside even though I've tried different strategies.

My ickiness can splinter into other feelings—envy, anger, shame, guilt, loneliness.
I just want the filth I feel to be gone.

I push others away.
I push You away.
God, to be honest, I fear You will receive me the way I receive myself—with rejection.
A part of me feels worse approaching or needing You at all.
I am tempted to beat myself up into doing better.
I don't want to be near me, You, or anyone at all.

But, God, I so desire to be clean.

Can Your love meet me even here?

God, let this ickiness be the inkling that connects me to You.
I won't resent my need to need You.
Instead, I open my needy heart to You.

This place I find myself is the very place You promise to meet me.
In my filth—You say *come.*
In my disgust—You say *stay.*
In my shame—You say *beloved.*

If I sinned, I say it.
If I was wrong, I say it.
If I don't even know why I feel the way I do, I say it.

Your love washes over my dirty soul.
You are relentless to pursue me even if I am running away.
You don't see me as detestable, but desirable.
You died so that You could be near me in my icky state.
You took on rejection so I don't have to.

I breathe.

You wipe my soul clean.
"Though your sins be as scarlet, they shall be as white as snow; though they be red like crimson, they shall be as wool" (Isaiah 1:18 KJV).

I let You come close.
I let You love me.
I let You stay beside me.

Even here, with how icky I feel, Your grace comes close to me. For this, I give You thanks.

Living Word

Your words are true. I will listen.

John 14:6
Jesus said to him, "I am the way, and the truth, and the life. No one comes to the Father except through me."

embarrassed

self-conscious, ashamed, or awkward

The Language for Feeling Embarrassed

I'm having a hard time forgetting the look on his face when I said what I said. I wasn't thinking when I blurted out an answer. He was appalled. Then he laughed. I should have known not to speak so quickly. I should have known not to show how little I actually knew. I should have known the answer. How could I not know it? Now I am stuck with that look he gave me. I felt so awkward. I didn't know what to say at the moment, so I laughed along with him. My secret was out.

Shame sneaks in. I feel uncomfortable. It messes with my already messy sense of self. I come undone when things I feel insecure about are exposed. I hate being seen through a lens I can't control. I made a mistake. It won't happen again. I'll make up for it. I'll be better next time. I am so tempted to cover the embarrassing thing I did. I am strategizing a way to undo it. I'll do anything to compensate for my foolishness. I would even go as far as to play dumb, pretend I'm fine, or lie. I don't want to feel my embarrassment so much that I will even leave the relationship. It's so hard to face the truth. I'd rather disengage or walk away.

For a moment, I let myself feel what I feel. I listen to my body, which holds my pain and my stories. My skin feels agitated. I want to hide. I notice the neurotic ways I want to deal with my feelings. My soul needs care right now. I need something I can't give myself. I want escape, but what I want more is for God to help me heal.

A Liturgy for When I Feel Embarrassed

Breathe in—*My Lord God . . .*
Breathe out—*cleanse my soul.*

I feel embarrassed.

I let myself feel what I feel.

Other feelings emerge—shame, disgust, ickiness, and agitation.

I feel my feelings emerge in my body.

Search my heart, God.

I cry out to You.

Reveal to me when I have felt this way in my story before.

God, my feelings are a signal to me that my soul needs more care.
I am so tempted to just cover up how I feel or run away.
I want to erase what happened and just move on.
But even if my body moves forward, my heart is still stuck in this moment.
Your love is the only thing that can cleanse my embarrassment.

God, help me discern if what I did was sinful.
If so, give me courage to make peace and receive Your compassion.
If my actions weren't sinful, help me set aside false shame that comes with sharp accusations.

God, I open my heart to You.

I let You see me as I am with all the icky and uncomfortable feelings.
I feel vulnerable because of the things I have done.
I don't want anyone to know.
I don't want anyone to see me.
I don't want to feel the way I do.

I wonder when in my story I have felt these feelings before.

I want to see myself honestly.

You invite me now to the well.
Here, Jesus, You know me and receive me.
Here, You give me fresh water for my soul.
Here, You reveal Your kindness toward me even in my shame.

At the well, You offer me living water.
This water satisfies me, but also sustains me.
This water exposes me but also cleans me.
Living water nourishes me.

At the well, my need is naked, but I am also safe.
I can be seen without having to hide.
I can be loved without having to prove.
I can be free without having to force anything.

When I feel the angst of my awkwardness—You give me water.

When I feel self-conscious and nervous about what I said or did—You give me water.

When I feel shame sticking to me—I timidly go to the water, where You await me.

You welcome me, want me, come beside me.

You know everything I've ever done, and You look upon me with eyes of compassion.

I look to You.

You say, "Blessed are the meek, for they shall inherit the earth" (Matthew 5:5).

God, You meet me in my embarrassment (meekness).
You not only cleanse me, You bless me.
You not only pursue me, You exalt me.
You not only love me, You lift me up.

Even in the filth that I feel, You offer more and more grace.

It is through my feelings of embarrassment that I encounter Your grace.

Here, I am loved.

Here, I am beloved.

Living Word

I pause to listen to You.

> ***John 4:13–15***
> Jesus said to her, "Everyone who drinks of this water will be thirsty again, but whoever drinks of the water that I will give him will never be thirsty again. The water that I will give him will become in him a spring of water welling up to eternal life." The woman said to him, "Sir, give me this water, so that I will not be thirsty or have to come here to draw water."

pressure

the suffocating feeling that comes with carrying the expectations of others

The Language for Feeling Pressure

I feel so much pressure. I can't escape it. The expectations are mounting. This pressure pulls me down. I have a hard time breathing. I must be strong. I must be attentive. I must carry it all. What others see isn't what is really happening inside of me. Inside of me I am cracking under this pressure to keep up. If I fail, others fall. The fear of that is hard. Inside I feel weak, fragile, and afraid. I keep going. I don't let others see my pain. I don't let anyone else get a glimpse of how bad I actually feel. Because on the inside, if

I really stopped to listen, I'd hear how unworthy I feel. I use my actions as a measuring stick to affirm my power, but really, I feel like I am on a merry-go-round I can't get off. So I keep managing the pressure. I ignore it by trying to beat it. I try to outrun it. I try to control it. I try tricks to minimize it like exercise, time management, or escaping reality by focusing on the future.

I'm tempted to give in to the pressure. I collapse. I so easily succumb to the voices and anxiety. When this happens, I turn to blame, accusations, and even anger. I don't like this about myself. I don't like that I snap at people I love.

For a moment, I make space to feel what I feel. As I stop, I feel the immensity of what I have been carrying. My body bears the weight of my emotional burdens. Boulders feel like they are being pressed down on me. My back and shoulders feel tight. I forget to breathe.

A Liturgy for When I Feel Pressure

Breathe in—*My Lord God . . .*
Breathe out—*help me find relief.*

I open my heart to You, God.

I feel pressure.

I pay attention to where I feel pressure in my body.

I want to be honest with myself.

Wher*e did I learn that I needed to carry everything?*

God, give me courage and curiosity to see why I do the things I do.

At some point, I believed I had the power to do things that You hadn't asked me to do.
Maybe I believed I could do it all.
Maybe I believed I *had* to do it all.

But as I stop, I am listening to what drives my pressure.

I believe it is my responsibility.
I must be enough.
I must be significant.
I must keep everyone safe.
I must be happy.
I must be right.
I must be strong.
I must be at peace.
I must . . .

God, this pressure exposes the deep beliefs of my heart.
Through this pressure, You want to purify my heart.
This pressure isn't to push me, but to purify me.
There is a purpose for it.

You are purging my soul of the lies that have led me here.
You want to release me from the expectations I live under.
You want to free me from my neurotic need to be God for everyone else.

I let this feeling be a siren that something in my soul needs care.
I listen to Your voice.
I let You lift my mounting expectations.

The truth is, I can't do anything without You.
I can't save, protect, help, control, make peace, gain approval, make things right, be strong, manage it all, or be enough without You.
But what I can do is let You attend to my deepest wounds.
I can let You be close to my heart and my fear of not carrying everything and everyone.

God, in this pressure and the fear of everything falling apart, I press into You.
I need Your help.
I can't do this alone.

Help untangle my story.

May I know in the deepest caverns of my soul that the only expectation You have for me is the expectation that I would receive Your love.

You love me when I do nothing at all.

Into Your hands, I place my life.
Into Your hands, I place the lives of those I love.
I trust that You care more about my life than I do.

Lord, hear my prayer.

Living Word

I want to hear what You have to say.

> ***1 Peter 5:6–7*** *NIV*
> Humble yourselves, therefore, under God's mighty hand, that he may lift you up in due time. Cast all your anxiety on him because he cares for you.

6

sadness

Sad—general sorrow

Pain—deep ache

Shame—the feeling of being bad

Depressed—experiencing deep, ongoing sadness

Discouraged—feeling dejection, despair, and disappointment

Fragile—the feeling that at any moment you could fall apart

Longing—desiring a life/person/things that you don't have yet or anymore

Hurt—being wounded

Tired—exhaustion

Invisible—feeling as though you aren't seen

Devastated—feeling that life as you knew it is over

Lonely—feeling alone

Rejected—not being wanted

Forgotten—abandoned

Sorrow—ongoing sense of grief

Gloomy—down, pessimistic, or bummed out

sad

general sorrow

The Language for Feeling Sad

She lay on her side. Her words were monotone and distant as though she were speaking into the void. "I'm afraid that if I let myself cry, I may never stop." And with those words, her tears came sliding, one by one, down off her cheek and onto the sheet. Beside her I lay quietly and breathed slowly. I was aware of each movement I made. No words were exchanged after that. She cried. I cried. We both wept until we fell asleep.

I confess I am tempted to dismiss my sadness. I measure my experiences against others' to determine whether my feelings are worthy to be felt. I know others have suffered more than I have. I don't want to be too emotional, so I minimize my pain. I can easily rationalize my feelings away. To be honest, I think I am just afraid to see how deep my sadness really is. I get upset when I can't control my tears. I don't want anyone else to see me. I want to speed up the healing process. At times, I am even drawn toward self-pity.

The truth is, I feel sad. It's dull and deep and rudely inconvenient. For a moment, instead of figuring out *why* I feel this way or if I *should* feel this way, I simply feel. I feel my heart hurting. I feel weighed down. I ache. I cry. I sweat. I feel anger, guilt, and helplessness too. I feel the fear that if I let myself be sad, the feeling may never stop. It feels endless.

Yet as I give myself to my sadness, it is a slight consolation that I am attending to the truth of my soul. This is where I find myself.

A Liturgy for When I Feel Sad

Breathe in—*My Lord God, help me receive . . .*
Breathe out—*help me release.*

God, I open my heart to You.

I feel sad. I feel it in my body.

I feel sadness now, but also in my story.

Search my heart, O God.

God, comfort me.

I cry out to You for help.

My heart aches with grief.

Disappointment fills my lungs. I ache with a throb that weighs me down. Sorrow wraps around my soul like a sickness with no cure.

I hurt.

In my tears, silence, song, words, slowness, or short breaths, I have to believe You are here.

In my ache, I resist my instinct to rationalize my sadness.
I resist my need to fix myself.
I resist the urge to speed up the process.

Even if the cause of my grief seems unimportant, You invite my sadness to come out. Even if my sadness is unorganized, messy, and incoherent, You invite me to open my heart to You.

Help me, God, to be curious about my sadness.

Help me, God, to be kind to my tender heart.

What is the root cause of my sadness?

I let all that I feel be felt. I give words to my tears.

I will speak.

I will listen.

I will trust.

You are the same God from yesterday.
You carried me through impossible valleys.
You never abandoned me in my despair.

You are the same God who holds the ocean today.
Like the tide, You give and take away.
Releasing and receiving is hard for me to do.

You are the same God of tomorrow.
You will go with me when unexpected sadness overcomes me.
You will make space for my soul to rest, weep, and lie down.

You are the same God who says, "Blessed are those who mourn" (Matthew 5:4).

Your nail-pierced hands beckon me to come.

My broken heart finds relief in Your broken hands.

You know sadness too.

Your Spirit helps my soul honestly pray, *Let it be so*.

Living Word

I will listen to You.

> ***Psalm 42:5–6***
> Why are you cast down, O my soul,
>   and why are you in turmoil within me?
> Hope in God; for I shall again praise him,
>   my salvation and my God.

pain

deep ache

The Language for Feeling Pain

The light is blinding. The noise of shuffling feet, muffled morning conversations, and buzzing from coffee brewing are already underway. Life is rising. I instantly feel a pang. Pain. I suddenly remembered what sleep could not shake. Dark memories shadow the hint of morning hope I had moments ago. Reality crashes in on me again. This gnawing ache is disabling me on the inside. It's hard to breathe. Life isn't as it was. Life will not ever be the same. This pain eats away at me like a monster. I turn over. The sheet is like a cocoon wrapping around my body. I go to my cave. I close my eyes. I don't hear anything but my affliction. I beg for sleep to take me back. I can't see anything but my pain. I am blinded, not by light this time, but by darkness. I feel pain.

I confess I don't want to open my heart. Doing such a thing hurts. I want to console myself by searching for the one person who can take my loneliness away. Life feels meaningless. I am tempted to avoid my pain and keep it quiet. I shift my pain from one place to another but try not to face it. I try to resolve my pain with busyness, distractions, and noise. I am also tempted to identify with my pain too deeply. My pain becomes my identity. I am tempted to believe that all I am is a victim of my pain. I begin to believe that this pain will never go away. I move to despair. The truth is I feel pain. I feel it in my body. It hurts everywhere. I don't know where to go from here. I don't know what to do. I don't want to feel this way anymore. I'll do anything to make this pain stop. I open my heart to God, even though I question His goodness.

A Liturgy for When I Feel Pain

Breathe in—*How long, O Lord . . .*
Breathe out—*must I feel this way?*

I feel pain. For a moment, I allow myself to feel what I feel.

I feel it in my body.

Reveal to me the story of my pain, O God.

God, my soul is close to anguish.

You are near.

This is the one place I have so badly not wanted to be.

Yet this is the place I find myself after much running, avoiding, and denial.

You have been waiting for me here.

The path behind me has been hard.
I see a road of loss, betrayal, breaking.
I see a road of loneliness, darkness, and despair.
I see a road that seems to have no end.

I know this road.

The path before me is also hard.

God, I don't want this path, yet there is no other way.
So I step forward.
I will walk it because You walked it before me.
You have walked the road of grief, fear, and sadness.
You know pain.

God, the only way out of pain is the way of the cross.
I may stumble, step, crawl, stand in rebellion, but I will set my gaze on the cross.
I will not take my eyes off the only hope I have left.

God, I don't like it, but I accept pain as my companion.
I walk through this pain.
As darkness closes in and I feel like I am alone—I lift my eyes to the cross.

God, I see You.
I see Your death and resurrection.
I see You forgiving those who harmed You.
I see You comforting the broken.
I see You caring for those You love.
I see You blessing those who cursed You.
I see You washing the feet of Your friends and betrayers.

You, God, see me and bid me *come*.

What You have done gives me courage to keep going.

God, I trust that You will provide a way through my pain so I can endure it.
You made a way for the Israelites in the desert with a pillar of fire—I trust You will help me see through the darkness too.

You gave Naomi a faithful daughter-in-law, Ruth—I trust that You will bring me help through a friend too.

You brought Simon of Cyrene to help when the cross was too much to bear—I trust that You will help me when I can't stand any longer.

My pain has a purpose. Pain is not the end of my story. Help me be curious about the origins of my pain. Help me be gentle with myself along the way. Help me be honest.

What did I need when my pain started?

What do I need now?

I let my soul lie bare before You.

In the quiet places of my pain, You care for me.
In my struggle, You remain close.

It is an intimacy I am oddly grateful for.
Perhaps I could never really know You or others if I never knew my pain.

As I walk the way of the cross, I am dying, but I am also coming alive.
As I walk out of darkness, I am waking up to something new.
Here, I am slowly becoming someone who I was always meant to be.
A person deeply rooted in love.
A person who is becoming free.

Even though my pain is painful, I also give You thanks because in a mysterious way, it allows me to find communion with You.

Living Word

Lord, help me listen to You.

> ***Romans 5:3–5***
> Not only that, but we rejoice in our sufferings, knowing that suffering produces endurance, and endurance produces character, and character produces hope, and hope does not put us to shame, because God's love has been poured into our hearts through the Holy Spirit who has been given to us.

shame

the feeling of being bad

The Language for Feeling Shame

I messed up again. I said words I can't take back and the bad in me was exposed. Something must be wrong with me. My mind races with justifications for my behavior. I was provoked. They were at fault. I warned them. But in the end, I was the one who lost control. I don't want to be this way. I don't want to be this kind of person. I feel so sad. I look for anything to make me feel better. I need something to replace my revealed flaws. I need something that will help me get away from . . . me. Sometimes it is subtle. Sometimes it screams. But my shame song haunts me like an annoying tune I can't stop singing. Like a sticky substance, shame leaves a residue on everything it touches in me. No distance can take me far enough away from my shame. No amount of my good can take away this feeling I have of being bad.

I feel uncomfortable. I am tempted to manage my feelings in isolation. No one knows I feel this way. I am good at covering up my bad with good. I do things to prove to others and myself that I'm not as bad as I feel. I easily move to self-justification, self-loathing, and self-hatred. I turn inward. I think things like, *I am bad, I am the worst, how could I, if anyone ever knew, I can't ever do anything right*. I internalize my shame as a weapon toward myself.

The truth is that I feel shame now. I feel it pulsing through my body.

My body tells the story of my shame. Though I try to escape my feelings or cover them up, shame is still strong inside of me. I know this.

I also know that God calls me out of shame and into freedom. I know this, although I have a hard time believing it. What do I do now? I feel stuck.

A Liturgy for When I Feel Shame

Breathe in—*Father God, help me . . .*
Breathe out—*receive grace.*

I feel shame.

I feel it in my body.

Soul, when did you learn you couldn't be loved in your shame?

This shame has long haunted me.
Confusion has rattled me.
Pain has afflicted me.

I've fought on the battlefield of my shame with great fervor, yet I've lost again and again.

In this place, I've felt embarrassed for not being better.
I've experienced humiliation and discomfort.
I have a deep longing not to live in the shadows of my mistakes, failures, and shortcomings forever.
Yet I am afraid there is no end.
Lurking in the fragile corners of my soul is sadness.
Here, I feel alone.

God, here, I cry out to You.
In the middle of my shame, I cry out to You.
In the middle of these uncomfortable feelings, I cry out to You.
In the middle of my attempts to hide my sin, I cry out to You, God.

Right here, as my heart trembles, You invite me into grace.
Grace to stop covering up.
Grace to stop trying harder.
Grace to stop cleaning up my bad.

God, grant me clarity to see my heart.
Is the shame I feel an indicator of my sin?
For the places I have sinned against You or another, forgive me.

God, is the shame I feel false shame (the neurotic need I have to fix myself)?

I open my heart to You, God.

Shame is an invitation to shift my gaze to grace.

To be honest, sometimes it is difficult for me to receive grace because it means I must face my inability to fix myself.
This is hard and easy.

It's hard because I am so prone to prove myself to others and even myself.
It is easy because my heart longs to be loved unconditionally.

Lord, help me receive grace even when my will wants to earn it. Help me receive my mistakes; simultaneously, help me receive Your invitation to grace.

Your grace comes after me like the father chasing after his Prodigal Son. Your grace comes after me like it did for the adulterous woman at the well.
Your grace comes after me the same way You pursued Peter after he denied You three times.

You peered into the eyes of Peter and asked, "Do you love me?"

Your grace moves toward me now and asks, "Do you believe that I love you?"

God, I want to say yes even though resistance still pulls me back. You ask me again and again until I can say yes with a full heart. Yes, I believe You really do love me.

Your love covers over all my shame.
Here, I am free.
My soul is clean.

I will give thanks to You all my days.

Living Word

God, I want to hear from You.

> ***2 Corinthians 5:21*** *NIV*
> God made him who had no sin to be sin for us, so that in him we might become the righteousness of God.

depressed

experiencing deep, ongoing sadness

The Language for Feeling Depressed

It was a very dark season of my life. The shades of my soul were pulled down tight. I don't remember much about that season, but I do remember the time I sat in my car motionless. My voice sounded muffled like I was underwater. My body slouched with the seatbelt coming up just below my chin line. *How did I get here?* I drove miles and miles without knowing it. *Where was I going?* I didn't think to call anyone. I didn't motion to move forward. I didn't want to do anything. I felt drained at the thought of trying to figure anything out. So I sat there. And the darkness of my heart matched the darkness of the sky. Lost, confused, hopeless, tired, sad, directionless, and desolate. *How long, O Lord, will I feel this way?*

A part of me didn't want to deal with my depression. I disliked it immensely. Another part of me wanted to deal with it on my own. I didn't want others nearby. I didn't want God. I felt trapped. I didn't want to be depressed. I wanted to be strong, capable, resilient, and rational. The shame I felt was intense and entangled me. I forced myself to keep going. Even though my body was moving, my heart was left behind. The more I tried to escape my deep sadness, the harder it became. I tried and failed. I tried and failed. I tried and failed.

The darkness pulled me under; my will wanted to fall asleep forever. I felt powerless. The weight was too much to bear. I isolated myself more and more. Thoughts of taking my life came and went. I imagined people and this world would be better off without me. I hated myself. The darkness was my only companion.

A Liturgy for When I Feel Depressed

Breathe in—*Father God . . .*
Breathe out—*help me.*

God, I open my heart to You.

I feel depressed. I feel it throughout my body.

Everything is dark.
I can't escape it.
I hate this pain, but I can't get away from it.
It is so deep, long, and wide.
It consumes me.

For a long time, I have lived under the intoxicating weight of anxiety.
It strangles me.
The lights have gone out.
It is hard to see hope.
Darkness pulls me under. It is all I see.
Depression pulls my soul under with the dead.
It suffocates me.

I feel alone. There is no way out, only down.
I am tired. I have lost all sense of joy, peace, and hope.
In many ways, I have lost contact with love.

I have wanted to die.

God, You spark a light within me that I am unable to ignite alone.

I am aware that evil can show up in my darkness as lies—*this will never end, God doesn't care about me, no one loves me, the world would be better off without me.*

Evil preys on my suffering and shame.
I use my remaining energy to cast out evil that manipulates my pain.
I pray with the psalmist, "Depart from me, all you workers of evil" (Psalm 6:8).

I may feel powerless, but I have the power to put a line in the sand.
No evil shall enter this space.
Sadness—yes.
Grief—yes.
Anger—yes.
But evil—no.

God, help me believe You are close to my pain.
You understand the agony of being human.
No other human could understand it more than You.
You were misunderstood, devastated, dehumanized, and betrayed.
You were left by brothers and abandoned by Your Father.
You cried out from the cross,
"'Eli, Eli, lema sabachthani?' that is, 'My God, my God, why have you forsaken me?'" (Matthew 27:46).
I borrow Your words—*where are You in this darkness, God?*
I cry out with You.
I cry out again and again.

God, I beg You to restore my hope.
Every breath is an act of my willingness to reach for hope.
My breath echoes in the tomb where You were buried—damp, quiet, cold.
I will wait here until Your morning light raises what is dead in me from the darkness.

Jesus, see me here and speak words of hope into my soul.
Your name, Jesus, is on my lips.

Living Word

God, I want to hear from You.

Psalm 6:6–9

I am weary with my moaning;
  every night I flood my bed with tears;
  I drench my couch with my weeping.

My eye wastes away because of grief;
 it grows weak because of all my foes.
Depart from me, all you workers of evil,
 for the Lord has heard the sound of my weeping.
The Lord has heard my plea;
 the Lord accepts my prayer.

discouraged

feeling dejection, despair, and disappointment

The Language for Feeling Discouraged

I didn't get the response I wanted. I was so excited to share my news, but my joy was met with skepticism and questions. I was bothered. I felt irritated. A rumbling inside of me persisted that I just couldn't manage or understand. A quiet aggravation. I continued moving about my day, but I felt a nagging feeling that I couldn't name. In all the movement, the sky caught my soul like a hook. I stopped. I looked up. As I did, air filled my lungs. Sadness rolled through me like a tumbleweed. Staggering and directionless. Ah, I knew this feeling. I felt discouraged.

I was tempted to get rid of it quickly. I dismissed it, rationalized it, and tried to forget about it by being busy and using false optimism. I was also tempted to give all my energy and attention to my emotions. I became moody and turned inward toward self-pity. My shame and self-condemnation felt heavy. *You never should have tried, you are a failure, no one cares* are thoughts that lodge in my mind.

For this moment, I allow myself to feel tired and sad. I notice that my body and spirit are weighed down. My attempts to rid myself of discouragement only entangle me more. I can't fix or resolve my feelings all alone. I need the company of God.

A Liturgy for When I Feel Discouraged

Breathe in—*Jesus, help me . . .*
Breathe out—*trust in You.*

God, I open my heart to You.

I feel discouraged. I feel it in my body.

I know this feeling holds meaning for me, so I pause to pray.
What I feel matters.
Things did not go the way I hoped they would go.

I am not where I thought I would be.
I am not where I want to be.
I am not where I should be.

God, my effort, work, and time have not paid off.
I feel let down.
I lack the courage to keep going.
But here I am.
I won't return to self-soothing or personal strength.
Instead, I will return to You.

God, this tender place I feel inside of me is where You are most present.
I believe that my discouragement is a back road to my becoming.
It is one way I can more deeply discover my profound belovedness.

This pathway is paved with many feelings, memories, and maybe even regret.
So, I feel.

I let the sorrow fill my senses.
Your Spirit leads me to the cross.

You know despair, dejection, and disappointment too.
You know the ache of things not going the way they should.
You know the longing for good while bad corrupts Your perfect creation.

In You, I find my solace.
In You, I find understanding.
In You, I find welcome.

Christ, may I learn from You.

In Your discouragement, You rested.
In Your discouragement, You prayed.
In Your discouragement, You fed Your soul on Scripture.

My grace is sufficient.

I lift my eyes up to the mountains.

You are the resurrection and the life.

You will finish what You started.

God, You lead me, through my discouragement, to the place where I am to be formed.
I want that.
I don't just want to *feel* better.
I want to become someone who *is* better.

God, use my current circumstances to develop in me greater faith, deeper trust, richer hope, and freedom from this sadness.

Despite all that I feel, still I will trust You.

I trust You with all the things I don't understand.
I trust You to hold my sadness with safekeeping.
I trust You to do the work that needs to be done in my life and in my soul.
I trust all things lead to my ultimate good and Your ultimate glory.

Into Your hands I place my life.

Thank You, Lord Jesus.

For even though this feeling aches within me, it is also through this feeling that I encounter Your love.

Living Word

I turn my heart to hear from You.

> ***2 Corinthians 4:16***
> So we do not lose heart. Though our outer self is wasting away, our inner self is being renewed day by day.

fragile

the feeling that at any moment you could fall apart

The Language for Feeling Fragile

I feel on edge. It has been days since the memorial service. The last of the out-of-town company has left. I am alone. Like the freezer crammed with frozen food, I feel my chest jammed up. I feel the chill of my own loneliness settling in. Everything seems to be triggering my tears. Everything inside of me feels shaky. I am hyperaware of my surroundings. I need to get out of here. I slip away. I come here. I come to my words that ground me. I explore my feelings and desperate need to hide. I feel out of control, tense, and a little sick. I feel fragile. I am tempted to try to fight how I feel. I gather my strength and try to regain my sturdiness. I push away, push through, or dismiss my feelings. I don't like feeling my weakness. I am even tempted to present myself as competent, capable, and powerful as a way to conceal my fragility.

Feeling my vulnerability makes me embarrassed. I can be self-critical. I believe that because I feel fragile, I *am* fragile. My fragility becomes my identity.

Even though it is uncomfortable, I let these feelings stay. I don't like feeling this way. I'm afraid that if I acknowledge these feelings, I will get stuck in them. I am afraid of where these feelings may lead me. I want to be different. I want to be better. I want another way. I want to be honest, real, and awake to God even when I feel so fragile.

A Liturgy for When I Feel Fragile

Breathe in—*Father, Son, and Holy Spirit, help me . . .*
Breathe out—*be made whole.*

I open my heart to You, God.

I feel fragile. I feel it in my body.

At some point I learned that feeling fragile was something I had to hide.
I'm afraid to be seen this way.
I'm desperate not to feel this way anymore.

God, I feel as if at any moment I could crack.
I'm trying to hold my life together.

I am trying to control uncontrollable things like people, circumstances, and outcomes.

But You, God, invite me to be with You.
You invite me to trust in Your goodness more than my strength.
You invite me, in my fragileness, to be spiritually formed.

I keep my heart open to Your love here.
I am in a tender place.
Here, I am moldable.
God, do Your soul work within me.
Fragility isn't my enemy, but it offers me the gift of growth.

God, through my fragileness Your light shines on my idols, sin, and shortcomings.
This makes me feel even more weak.
But instead of turning inward, I unfold my soul before You.

I set the eyes of my heart on the cross.
With my finger I trace and retrace the cross on my palm.
At the cross, my fragility comes in contact with Your great strength.

God, in ways I cannot see, You are helping me become whole.
You are piecing me back together.
You are healing me at the cross.
You are forming me out of something old, into someone new.

I trust that You, God, are forging in me something good.
I trust that You will take all the sharp ends of my soul and shape in me softness.
I trust that the splintered places in me will all be sewn into a garment for glory.

Though fragility feels painful, it also becomes a funnel through which Your grace and love can reach me. Because of this, my heart will forever praise You.

Living Word

God, Your child is listening.

> ***Isaiah 42:3***
> A bruised reed he will not break.

longing

desiring a life/person/things
that you don't have yet or anymore

The Language for Feeling Longing

"What do you want?" She looked directly at me. She wasn't asking me for my lunch order. She was asking me for my dreams. I let this question settle in. It sank like lead in water to the bottom of my soul. Immovable. *What do I want?* I am a little annoyed by the question. I'm afraid to ask. I am afraid to feel the canyon of longings inside of me. If I were to step toward the edge of my desires, I might not be able to resurface. So I pull myself back. I draw my arms tight around my dreams like a life vest. I dare not speak, for the whisper of things longed for might betray me. I shake myself awake to the present. "What do I want?" I pause. "I want a nap." I chuckle. My laughter deflects the question, and my dream dies once again.

I feel longings. I am tempted to shut down any echo of desire. I strategize my life in such a way that I pursue what I want while simultaneously trying not to get hurt. I am also tempted to make my life all about the fulfillment of others' longings. When my longings emerge, they can consume me. They take over my imagination. I can't stay present to reality. They become so powerful that I can't think about anything else.

The truth is, I have deep longings. They rise up within me. I can feel them in my body now, and they make me sad.

At times I forget my desires. At other times, they torment me. At this moment, I just let myself feel what I feel. My heart feels sick. My desires have lain dormant for so long. Where do I go from here?

A Liturgy for When I Feel Longing

Breathe in—*Jesus, help me . . .*
Breathe out—*trust You.*

I feel longings.

I feel desires within me, and my body reacts.

I pay attention to how I receive or reject my longings.

God, this is where I find myself, and I ache.

For a moment, I allow myself to feel what I feel.

When I have the courage to look intently at my longings, I find where my heart really is.
Like a mirror, longings never lie.
Filters lie. Photographs lie. Smiles lie. People lie. I lie.
But longings—they always tell the truth.
My longings don't tell me what to do but tell me what I want.

God, my sorrow is close to me.
Sadness can be a hard feeling for me because I fear there is no end.
Yet here, comfort also awaits me.
Comfort from You and comfort from letting myself feel what I really feel.

God, I question if my desires even matter.
I've nearly forgotten some.

Some of my longings were once loud, but as hope faded and pain endured, it seemed like the best choice I had was to let them go. I may have convinced myself that the quieter my longings were, the less they could hurt me.

God, sometimes my longings overpower me.
I feel them, see them, and can almost touch them.
I see others with the very thing I long for most in life.
In my longings, I feel my grief.
I feel the gap between where I am and where I want to be.
I feel the distance between my reality and what seems like an unreachable dream.

Father in heaven, You invite me to pray honestly.
You make room for my longings to live.
You make a safe space for me to feel.
You make a way for my dreams not to die in the dark.

God, I touch my longings with vulnerable faith.
Like the sick woman in Luke 8:43–48, I reach out to You.
I reach out with just a pinch of hope that You can make all things well.
You alone can meet me in the very depths of my longings, secret dreams, and whispered desires.
You are with me in my ache.

My longings become my soul's song.
Pain is the melody; hope is the harmony.
They don't compete, but rather complement each other.
They are my heart's hum; they remind me that my life is woven together with complexities that don't fracture me but form me.

I don't run ahead.
I don't turn back.
I don't get swallowed up by sadness.
I sigh forward.

God, I lean into my longings with You.
I trust that whatever may come, will come.
With this, a wellness settles within my soul.

For even in my longings, You gather me in and greet me with love.
Here, with You, my longings find reprieve.

Living Word

God, I tune my heart to hear from You.

Proverbs 13:12 *NIV*
Hope deferred makes the heart sick,
but a longing fulfilled is a tree of life.

hurt

being wounded

The Language for Feeling Hurt

It was impossible not to notice that I was the only one not included. He was there. She was there. They were all invited but me. Whether or not that is true, it feels true. Pain inside of me is pricked. I scroll on, but my soul is stunned by what I saw. Laughter, connection, and relationships are being formed without me. Something inside of me aches. I feel hurt. Life is changing. Things are shifting. I can't find my balance.

Out of my sadness, I want to steamroll my feelings. I push my feelings aside and dismiss them. I project my pain onto others. I become angry. A dark part of my soul wants others to suffer. I turn inward on my hurt. I just want to give up, curl up, not care, mope, beat myself up.

For this moment, I let my hurt take up all the space. I let my hurt stay. I notice how it affects my body. I notice how it stews in my thoughts.

I notice how it swirls in my chest. My hurt feelings can easily keep me from the one thing my soul needs the most, the care and love of God.

A Liturgy for When I Feel Hurt

Breathe in—*Jesus, help me . . .*
Breathe out—*with this hurt.*

I feel hurt.

God, I open my heart up to You.

I can spend much of my time wondering if I *should* feel hurt.
I think this is one way I avoid actually feeling the hurt I have.
I set aside bossy voices inside of me dictating whether I should or should not feel what I feel.
Instead, I allow myself to be where I am.

I refuse to wrangle my heart as though it is a problem to solve.
I resist logically trying to find an answer.
I won't replay the situation over and over.

Instead, Lord, I open my hurt feelings to You.
You invite me to feel the depth, breadth, and width of what my soul is experiencing.

God, I am hurt.

Perhaps life is changing, and this is hard.

Perhaps I was missed, rejected, or neglected.

Perhaps I am still grieving.

Reveal to me, God, where my pain really resides.

I make room for honest reflection.

Help me be soft with my sadness.
In the deep waters of my heart, God, You are with me.
You know the specific reasons for my ache.
You dwell in my heart.
You dwell where my pain is.
You know my loneliness.
You know my loss.

How, Lord, do You attend to me in my pain?

God, search my heart.

Grant me the grace to attend to my soul with compassion.

Grant me the courage to give my sadness words.

Grant me the wisdom to know that sorrow is the way of healing.

God, You attend to my hurt with nourishment, assurance, and kindness.

As You cared for the hurting, You care for me.
You make space.
You pull out a chair at the table.
You invite me to grieve.
You are in no rush.
You listen to all my stories of hurt.

I entrust my wounds into Your wounds.
God, would You heal up my hurt in Your good time?
Help me be patient with the slow work You are doing in me.

Even here, through my feeling of being hurt, I marvel at how my pain becomes a pathway to prayer.

Thank You for not leaving me alone to navigate my hurt feelings on my own. Rather, You reveal my hurt as a way to bring me deep, healing peace.

For this, I give You thanks.

Living Word

I turn my heart to hear from You.

> ***Psalm 139:1–3***
> O Lord, you have searched me and known me!
> You know when I sit down and when I rise up;
> you discern my thoughts from afar.
> You search out my path and my lying down
> and are acquainted with all my ways.

tired

exhaustion

The Language for Feeling Tired

I wash my hands. With reluctance, I peek at my reflection. Instantly, I regret it. *This is me.* I bring my finger to my face. I slip loose hair behind my ear as though this gesture could cure a lifetime of bad hair days. Dark circles sadly sink like upside down rainbows under my eyes. The longer I look, the more weariness rises up inside of me. I try to catch my breath, but as I do, I feel the weight of my exhaustion. It's heavy like a boulder weighing me down. I find myself slumped over the sink. Those stubborn strands of hair swing down across my face again. If I could, I would collapse onto the bathroom floor and cry. In the distance I hear a faint call. I am needed. I have to keep going. With fortitude

I pin my rebellious bangs back into my bun like fastening a seatbelt. I have to go.

I feel tired. I feel sad. I feel alone. Sometimes I even ignore how tired I really am. I treat my body like it is a machine. No one gives me extra credit for this. I just do it. I just push on and press forward. Sometimes I try to garner sympathy for my tiredness. I want ongoing affirmation for all I do. At times, I can drown in my feelings to the point where I stop doing what I ought to be doing. My shame is loud here—*What's wrong with me? Why can't I keep up? Am I a failure for feeling this way?*

I am tired physically, mentally, and spiritually. I am exhausted. For a moment, I let my tiredness set in. I let it fill my body. I pay attention to how it shows up in me. Whether I should or shouldn't be tired is irrelevant. The reality is that I am. My body, soul, mind, and spirit are drained. I let it be so. I open my heart to God.

A Liturgy for When I Feel Tired

Breathe in—*Jesus, help me . . .*
Breathe out—*find my rest in You.*

God, I come to You bearing my soul.

I feel tired. I feel it in my body. I've known this feeling in my story.

I need Your gentleness now because I am prone to push and punish myself.
I need Your kindness because many voices crowd my mind.
I need Your hospitality because I have a hard time welcoming myself with all of my needs.

God, I come to You.
You invite me to lay down my load.
One by one, I do.

I lay down my people.
I lay down my tasks.
I lay down my responsibilities.

I lay down my pride.
I lay down my time.
I lay down my results.
I lay down my fears.
I lay down all the possibilities.
I lay down my expectations.
I lay down my tidiness.
I lay down my rights.

I lie down.

God, help me rest.

I am not just one of the flock.
I am Your sheep.
One whom You know by name.
One whom You have called beloved.
One whom You've blessed with breath.

I come.
I exhale.
I rest.

I allow myself to be received like a sheep to its shepherd.
I fall limp over Your shoulders.
I lay all of me and all of my burdens onto Your back and trust that You will not let the enemy strike me down.

You are patient.
You are kind.
You are good.
You are gentle.
You are peace.
You are humble.

As I come, I let You love me.
As I come, I let You carry.

I come into Your heart that is unhurried, unbothered, unafraid.

I come with my tears.
I come with my loss.
I come with my pain.
I come with my sorrow.

I come into Your rest.

Amen.

Living Word

May I hear Your words for me.

> ***Matthew 11:28–30***
> Come to me, all who labor and are heavy laden, and I will give you rest. Take my yoke upon you, and learn from me, for I am gentle and lowly in heart, and you will find rest for your souls. For my yoke is easy, and my burden is light.

invisible

feeling as though you aren't seen

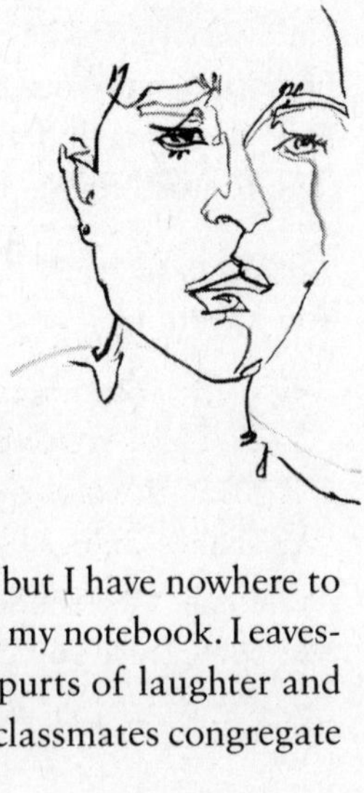

The Language for Feeling Invisible

I'm wearing my vibrant joggers and gray sweatshirt. With my hair tied up effortlessly in a tasseled bun, I sit on the picnic table. The campus is bustling with students and staff. Groups mingle while walking from class to class. I sit trying to look busy, but I have nowhere to go and nothing I have to do. I fumble through my notebook. I eavesdrop on conversations walking by. I catch spurts of laughter and chatter as college kids sip on coffee. Fellow classmates congregate near me. Their circle is tight and intent on keeping the gateway closed to newcomers. I am with others, but no one sees me. I feel invisible.

I don't want to deal with my feelings. Now I almost don't want to be seen. I want to avoid my sadness because I am afraid of it. I protect how I really feel. I work, act, and do so many things as a way to be seen. I put on something (clothing, actions, humor, achievements) as a way to feel more real. I feel unknown. I don't want to feel this feeling, so I hide more. I silence my voice, disappear, blend in more, go further into the distance. I immerse myself in my feelings as though they have the final say. Because I feel unknown, I believe that no one wants to know me.

I feel invisible. I let these feelings stay. My body feels off.

I feel unseen. I feel sad. I don't want to try anymore. This is a hard feeling to feel. Where is God? *El Roi*, You are the God who sees.

A Liturgy for When I Feel Invisible

Breathe in—*Jesus, Lord and Savior, help me . . .*
Breathe out—*walk this road.*

I feel invisible.

God, I open myself to You.

I have felt this way before. My story is filled with this feeling.

Many moments have led me to this moment.
My voice wasn't heard.
My thoughts weren't valued.
My feelings weren't acknowledged.
My sadness hangs like an invisibility cloak over me.
So few people really know me.
The ache is deep.

Lord, where am I?

Even though people are around me, I can feel alone, as though I am in a desert.
I feel isolated.
I feel unknown.
I feel lost with my longings.

Lord, I am tired of looking for affirmation, connection, and something solid to stand on.
I am tired of figuring out what it means to be real.
I am tired of searching to be seen.
I am tired of hoping I'll be wanted.
I am tired of trying.

Lord, is it possible that this desert place is the way You have led me?
Is this place where I find myself part of my journey?
Is this the way I will be found?

The way You found the Israelites was through the desert.
The way You found Moses was in the desert.
The way You found Hagar was in the dry, murky, dusty brown, and endless desert.
It was in the desert that they finally faced themselves and You.

Lord, no more wandering.
No more searching, trying, hunting, or hustling.
No more trying to fit in.
No more trying to stand out.
No more trying to fix myself as though I were a problem to solve.
No more.

Lord, instead I step on this dry land.
I face my fear.
I face my sadness.
I face my shadows.
I face You.

Lord, I will go down this desert road.
It is one You know well.
It is one where You fasted for forty days.

It is one where You faced Your humanness.
It is one where You went unseen as well.
It is one in which You were tempted three times by Your enemy.

Lord, this desert road is one that led You to the cross.
It includes hardship.
It requires great honesty and faith.
It includes death but leads to life.

Lord, as You lead me, I will follow.
I believe this desert place of feeling invisible is the way in which my flesh will be seen and my soul will be satisfied.

I pray it is so.

Living Word

God, I want to hear from You.

> ***Genesis 16:13***
> So she called the name of the Lord who spoke to her, "You are a God of seeing," for she said, "Truly here I have seen him who looks after me."

devastated

feeling that life as you knew it is over

The Language of Feeling Devastated

The fluorescent lights sear down on me. My body lies limp on the stone-cold medical table. I don't understand anything the doctor is saying. All I see are his compassionate eyes that speak kindness but waver with warning. I can see his fear. I am in danger. Without any outside help, without rescue or more medical care, there isn't much he can do. And in a moment, everything changes. Hope gone. I can hardly breathe. I feel devastated.

I am desperate to control the circumstances any way I can. At moments, I feel like a fighter. I work so hard to change, manage, and fix the circumstances so that the pain will go away. I work hard to make things better, change the outcome, or figure out what went wrong. At other times, I feel like I don't have any fight left in me. The darkness has taken over me. I see no way out. There is no light, life, or way out of this but to be buried under the reality. All the air is gone.

It is impossible to comprehend how utterly devastated I feel.

So, for this moment, I let the pain stay without moving to action. I just feel. The feeling is suffocating. My body is heavy with loss. I have lost so much. I have so much left to lose. O God, my God, turn Your face to me.

A Liturgy for When I Feel Devastated

Breathe in—*God* . . .
Breathe out—*hear my prayer.*

I feel devastated.
I feel it in my body.
I open my heart to You.

God, *how*?

How did things end up this way?
How have I lost what I held so dear?
How can I go back in time?
How can I make sense of tomorrow?

God, now . . .

Now, I am left with darkness.
Now, I am left with confusion.
Now, my soul is in anguish within me.

God, hurry . . .

Hurry and make things better.
Hurry and heal this great chasm inside of me.
Hurry and answer my prayers because I grow impatient easily.

God, help . . .

Help me know what to do.
Help me know where to go.
Help me know what to say.

God, hear . . .

Hear my cry from the pit.
Hear my agony as night descends on my life.
Hear my desperate desire to not feel this way.

God, make . . .

Make a way for me to wait that is bearable.
Make a way to endure this pain.
Make a way for me to believe another life is possible.

God, I . . .

I trust You will speak when You need to speak.
I trust You will answer me when an answer is needed.
I trust that You will protect me.
I trust that You will not leave me here forever.

God, You . . .

You are my shelter.
You are my hiding place.
You are the beginning and end.
You are the maker of heaven and earth.
You are the overseer of things.
You are my hope.

God,

So much grief resides in me.

So much pain punches down on me.
So much loss is left to feel.
And yet, You know this darkness I speak of as well.
In this, I take comfort.
Even here, I am not alone.

You meet me here.

O God, who have I left but You?

Living Word

I incline my heart to hear from You.

> ***Psalm 88:1***
> O Lord, God of my salvation,
> I cry out day and night before you.

lonely

feeling alone

The Language for Feeling Lonely

I pull the handles of the refrigerator doors open. The white light makes me blink in contrast to the darkness around me. I squint forward. My eyes search the shelves. I trace through all the random ingredients and leftovers, looking for something I can make. Nothing. But I still stand there. I am looking for something, but I don't know what exactly. I want to consume, take in, taste. The bleakness in the fridge mocks me. I swing the doors shut. I feel empty. My eyes scan my soul. Like connecting the dots, I start to see something emerge from nothing. This isn't hunger. This is loneliness.

This is a painful feeling. I don't like it. I am tempted to fill my loneliness with anything and everything. I search for objects, people, or pleasure to fill the void inside of me. I turn toward anything to find reprieve. I even use good things to try to fix my pain (exercise, busyness, hobbies, work, parenting, service). I am tempted to let my loneliness have power over me. I oversleep. I don't really engage in my life. I don't take care of myself or my responsibilities. I pull back, isolate, and resign myself to days of letting my loneliness consume me. I feed my loneliness with self-pity. I believe that I am the only one who feels this way.

The truth is, I feel lonely. I can trace it throughout my story. I have experienced lonely love. Even when I have been loved by people, I have still felt unknown by them. If I look carefully, it has always been lurking inside of me. For a moment, I have the courage to see it and feel it. Something deep in me aches. I pay attention to the ways my body reacts to my loneliness. In all my attempts to deal with my loneliness, I can't rid myself of it. I have to believe there is another way through it.

A Liturgy for When I Feel Lonely

Breathe in—*Jesus, help me . . .*
Breathe out—*be filled by Your love.*

God, I open my heart to You.

I feel lonely.
I feel it in my body.
I know this feeling from my story.

I have been eating the food of entertainment that offers false fulfillment.

I have been devouring the drink of influence, power, and control that promised to pay me back with significance but left me parched.

I have been sipping on the wine of work, affection, and good behavior that has left me thirsty for more.

I have sat at the table of stuffing my body with outside pleasure for so long, only to be left starved.

Yet my anxiety to fill myself up always returns.
Each attempt to fill my loneliness has just been pain management.

God, here I find myself again, afraid to feel what I actually feel.

Give me curiosity to see when and where my loneliness began. Give me courage to face it. Give me kindness and compassion toward myself as You are kind and compassionate toward me.

I want to be deeply known and loved.

God, You have been inviting me into my loneliness.
You are inviting me to be known.

This lonely me is who You have always loved.
This lonely me is who You left heaven to lift up.
This lonely me is who You died to rescue from darkness.
This lonely me is who You seek out to save not just once, but throughout my ongoing story.

This lonely me is who You want to know right now.

Fill in the shadows and fill in the shame.
Fill in what is shattered and what is splintered.
Fill in what is barren and what is blank.
Fill in what is hollow and what is hurting.
Fill in what is desolate and what is dark.

I wait.
My soul waits for You to fill me in.
In You, I am fully known.

Even though this feeling of loneliness aches within me, it is also the way in which I come into Your grace. Loneliness is the pathway to Your presence.
For this, I give You thanks.

Living Word

You respond to me with words of love, and I will listen.

> ***John 6:35*** *NIV*
> Then Jesus declared, "I am the bread of life. Whoever comes to me will never go hungry, and whoever believes in me will never be thirsty."

rejected

not being wanted

The Language for Feeling Rejected

"I'm done. I've closed the door. It is what it is." I can't get these words you said to me out of my head. I rehearse and replay the conversation over and over. I think of all the things I want to say to you. I check my phone. *Maybe I missed a text.* Nothing. I put down my phone. Without any effort at all, a fantasy plays out in my imagination. It always has the same ending. You come back to me full of regret, apologies, and the desire to reconnect.

Everything in me feels heavy. How do I live with this pain? I can hardly breathe. It hurts. I can't imagine life without you. I get ready for the day. But this ache makes it hard to move. I feel angry. I feel confused. I feel misunderstood and shattered. I feel bothered that I care so much. I hate how you have this hold on me. I gather my things and head to the car. I get in. I check my phone again, *just in case.* Nothing. I slam the car door harder than necessary. You're the one who closed the door. Nothing I can do will open it. I start the engine. I start to cry.

I feel rejected. I feel alone. I am tempted to reject my feelings. I push my feelings down. I have tried to adjust and change myself for the sake of simply belonging. I want to reject those who have rejected me. I am also prone to reject myself—*What is wrong with me? Maybe I have a fault that I can't see. Maybe I did something that keeps me on the outside. My lack of belonging is because I am somehow broken.* These feelings and thoughts overpower and immobilize me. I am tempted to reject others before they have rejected me.

For a moment, I stay with my feeling of rejection. I feel the horrible weight of this feeling. I have a deep longing to belong, to be wanted, to be desired. I feel this feeling in my body as a stinging ache. My eyes search for belonging and my mind strategizes ways to get it. All my attempts to rid myself of this feeling have been unsuccessful.

There must be another way.

A Liturgy for When I Feel Rejected

Breathe in—*Jesus, help me . . .*
Breathe out—*find my acceptance in You.*

I open my heart to You now.

I feel rejected. I even feel it in my body.

Allow me to see the places in my story where I have experienced this feeling before.

I want to be received.
This feeling is painful.
Sadness like this stings deep within me.

I bring all of my rejected parts to You.

My feelings of rejection are a sign that my soul longs for true connection.

God, I walk into my feelings instead of fighting them or fleeing from them. I walk into my rejection the way You walked into Yours, with courage and conviction.
As I walk into the wilderness with desolation, heartache, and confusion, I am also walking into hope, belonging, and my true home.

Love can be found here.
I can find love on the outskirts, margins, and fringes.

In my rejection—*I accept that I am powerless to make my life possible.*

In my rejection—*I accept that I am powerless to control others.*

In my rejection—*I accept that I am powerless to make others love me.*

In my rejection—*I accept that You fully accept and want me.*

God, even in this sadness, You welcome me the way You welcomed the little children, the sick, and the poor, the wealthy, the wandering, and the lost. Even in my rejection, You offer me bread that satisfies and water that soothes.
Even here, when I feel alone, make a way through the pain so I can bear it.

I can't endure this alone.

I need a reminder that You have not lost sight of me.

I need a glimmer of hope that You have good for me beyond this.

I need to know that today, I will be okay even when I don't feel that way.

May it be through this heartache that I discover deeper dimensions of Your love for me.

Lord, hear my prayer.

Living Word

I incline my heart to hear from You.

Psalm 27:10
For my father and my mother have forsaken me,
but the Lord will take me in.

forgotten

abandoned

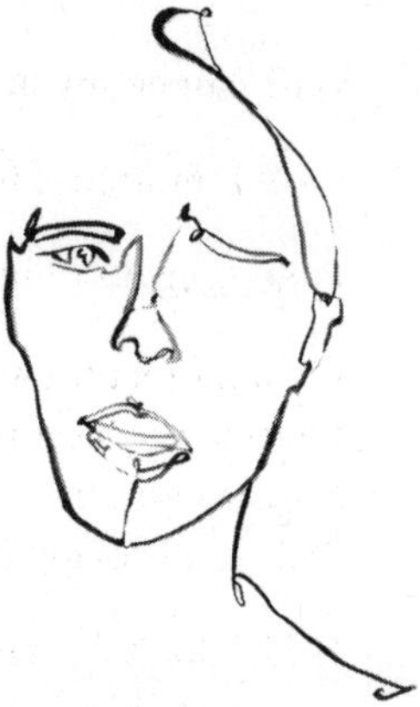

The Language for Feeling Forgotten

I try not to glance up at the stands. I dare not confirm my faint suspicion. I can't help myself. I look. Seats packed with people, but vacant of the one person I hoped would be present. I come straight back here to the court. With aggression I go after the game. With power I push back what I really feel. I play harder. And the war inside me rages. The pain pulls me apart. I leave you no excuse to leave me. The end. The sea of fans sings a chant of praises and I go to my car in silence. Nothing changes. I'm alone again. I get in my car. I turn up my music to tune it all out. I drive away. I leave myself behind the way you left me. I feel forgotten.

I do not like feeling this way. It triggers trauma inside of me from my past. I tend to use people, causes, or activities to fill the void of my pain. I push through feelings because they hurt too much. I use my power to push aside or push through what I feel. I believe that I am responsible for other people leaving me. I feel shame, self-hate, slothfulness, and self-pity.

The truth is, I hurt inside. I'm sad inside. I stay with these feelings of forgottenness. Before I react, I stay. I allow my feelings of abandonment to rise up within me. My body feels the weight of my feelings. Nothing I do seems to erase the abandonment sealed in my story. What else can I do now?

A Liturgy for When I Feel Forgotten

Breathe in—*Jesus, help me . . .*
Breathe out—*be Your child.*

God, I open my heart to You.

I feel forgotten. I feel this in my body.

How long, O Lord, will I feel this way?

For a moment, I allow myself to feel my feelings.
From my earliest memories or just recently, I felt left behind.
I was forgotten by people who were meant to care for me.
Instead of loving me with their presence, they were absent.

God, I don't want to live with this feeling of forgottenness anymore.
You invite me to be fathered by You.
This is a divine calling.
As Your child, I can run into Your room at any hour.
As Your child, I have unfettered access to Your side table.
You will never leave me, send me away, or make me prove that my presence matters.

God, You invite me to be mothered by You.
Here, You tend to my wounds.
Here, You keep safe watch over me.
Here, You welcome, delight in, and celebrate my presence.

God, You invite me to be sistered and brothered by You.
Here, I fully belong.
I sit with a table of brothers and sisters who know not only my name but my pain.
In the church I find communion with sojourners just like me.
Here there are sinners and saints who were orphaned too.
Here, You restore my family.

God, You invite me to walk.
I walk on this dim road of healing with You.
I don't stray to the left and depend on what others say or think.
I don't lean to the right by giving my worth away to the one who left me.

I don't depend on myself for my own strength.

I walk in faith that my abandonment story is leading to full adoption.

God, You invite me to trust.
I trust that this isn't the end of my story.
I trust that You will never lose sight of my coming and going.
I trust that You seek after me like You sought after the lost sheep, the lost coin, the lost son.
I trust that You ultimately seek my good because I am Your child.

May I not just know that I belong to You, but may I truly come to believe it as well.

Lord, You hear my prayer.

Lord, You see my life.

Lord, You restore my soul.

Living Word

I will listen to You.

Romans 8:13–17 *NIV*

For if you live according to the flesh, you will die; but if by the Spirit you put to death the misdeeds of the body, you will live.

For those who are led by the Spirit of God are the children of God. The Spirit you received does not make you slaves, so that you live in fear again; rather, the Spirit you received brought about your adoption to sonship. And by him we cry, "*Abba*, Father." The Spirit himself testifies with our spirit that we are God's children. Now if we are children, then we are heirs—heirs of God and co-heirs with Christ, if indeed we share in his sufferings in order that we may also share in his glory.

sorrow

ongoing sense of grief

The Language for Feeling Sorrow

I miss you. I can't remember not feeling this way. A coat of sadness covers my soul. Sometimes my grief pricks and pokes me, while other times it is soft and almost soothing. Today it came on with a fierce kick. I saw someone else celebrating something I'll never get to celebrate, and the pins holding my heart in place snapped. Tears everywhere. The irrevocable loss I have feels like it will never heal. Here I go again. Here hopelessness sneaks in and whispers lies—*You'll never get better. You'll always feel this way. There is no good left for you. People are tired of your pain.* I sew my soul back up with the little remaining thread I have left. I curl into myself. My coat returns. But it doesn't comfort me this time. Instead, it keeps people out; I keep myself turned in.

I feel great sorrow. At times I resist feeling what I feel. I am tempted to respond to my sadness by running away from it or fighting it. I want it gone. I am tired of feeling this way. Even in laughter, my heart feels a sting. My face wears strength, but my soul is weary. I turn inward, believing there is no way out. I've let sorrow become a part of my identity. I believe it will never end. Instead of claiming my sorrow, I let my sorrow have claim over me. I have tried so many things to make this feeling go away, yet my sorrow feels wed to my soul.

For a moment, I let this wave of sadness stay. I feel it in my body. It swells in me. Tears fall. More tears are to come. This feeling is so familiar. I long for there to be a way through this sadness that doesn't crush me but cures me.

A Liturgy for When I Feel Sorrow

Breathe in—*Jesus, my good shepherd . . .*
Breathe out—*comfort me now.*

I open my heart to You.

I feel sorrow.

I feel it in my body.

I trace the story of my sorrow and allow You, God, to lead me to what pain needs to be grieved in me right now.

Even here, disappointment meets me.

I am not where I want or hoped I would be.

I feel this sadness well up within me.

I let myself be sad.
I let myself grieve.
I express my sorrow with tears, sighs, and even silence.
You say the one who grieves is the one who will be lifted up.
My sadness becomes access to my comfort.

My sorrow is a doorway to the Man of Sorrows. "He was despised and rejected by men, a man of sorrows and acquainted with grief; and as one from whom men hide their faces he was despised, and we esteemed him not" (Isaiah 53:3).

Jesus, You know the long road of intense loss.
You know grief, rejection, loss, emptiness, betrayal, and humiliation. Jesus, You understand what it is like to walk in the shadow of grief while existing in the land of the living.

Jesus, will You lift me up as You were lifted?

From grave to glory, will You wrap my wounds in the comfort of Your care?
From grief to goodness, will You bind my sorrow in Your holy robe?
From gloom to growth, will You hide my pain in the hole of Your healing hand and restore in me new life?

Jesus, help me endure this wave of sadness.

Remind my soul of what my mind knows: that this grief will not swallow me but pass through me.

I need Your words of comfort now.

Even though sorrow seems to slow me down, it is the way Your love seeps into my soul. I enter my river of sorrow. I will not resist the water, but move with it. As I do, I come into Your love.

Comfort me now, O Lord, that my sadness may find a home in You.

Lord, hear my prayer.

Living Word

God, I listen to You. I believe that what You say is true.

> ***Matthew 5:4***
> Blessed are those who mourn, for they shall be comforted.

gloomy

down, pessimistic, or bummed out

The Language for Feeling Gloomy

I felt off today. To be honest, I didn't even notice I was feeling this way until I was falling asleep. While tossing and turning, I started to name what was conspiring in my heart. I feel down. I feel sad. Winter is rolling in with her early and dark curtain call to each day. The chill moves in like a coastal fog. I am cold. I notice that when I don't see the sun, my heart feels distress. With this new season, I said good-bye to rhythms I love. I love the warmth of autumn. I love late evenings. I love the kids' activities and the friends we see at the field. But that season is gone now. A brief sadness has come across me.

This feeling is so slight that I am tempted to gloss over it. It is easy for me to just keep going. But as my heart snags within me, I try to listen. I listen to my sadness. I listen to what I may need to let go of. I listen to my body. I let my gloominess stay. Perhaps God has something for me here to pay attention to.

A Liturgy for When I Feel Gloomy

Breathe in—*My Lord my God . . .*
Breathe out—*You sustain my soul.*

I open my heart to You, God.

I feel gloomy. I feel it in my body.

I'm not sure what to do with my sadness today. Give me wisdom to know what in my heart needs to be processed and prayed.

My gloominess comes and goes like the fog.

I feel the ache move through me.
I feel loss snagging my soul.
I feel hesitant to camp here too long.

But I am here now, and I trust that You care about my life. As insignificant as my sorrow may be, I believe that You care.

Life is changing.
Seasons come and go.
I can't hold anything still.
I can't control the passage of time.

I refrain from thinking my feelings.
Instead, I feel them, hold them, and acknowledge them.
I unfold my heart to You.

I don't need to edit my words or feelings with You, God.

In this place, You are my constant.

Your Spirit sorts through my spirit.
Your Spirit comforts my spirit.
Your Spirit consoles and welcomes me to come undone.

Though sadness exists even when words do not, I trust You will bring me understanding.
Though I can't shake this feeling, I trust that You are unshaken by it.
Though I can't make sense of all my circumstances, I trust that You will make straight my path in due time.

As the seasons change, so do my feelings.
I wait on You.
I wait on the premise that this is not the end.
I wait on the promises of Your love to see me through.

I know this feeling isn't final, but a passage place.
It is a place I must move through in prayer.
It becomes holy ground for hope to transpire.
You are with me in this liminal space.

I trust that even here, You are forming my heart in love.
Help me see what I need to let go of.
Help me see what to hold on to.
Once again, I entrust my life and the lives of those I love into Your care.

As life changes, I believe with all of my being that You desire my good.
Even here, You are forming my heart.
The growing pains I feel now are growing me to be one who loves as I have been loved.

As I feel my moods swing and sway, I lean on You.
I allow my sadness to be the space where Your love welcomes me to come undone.

Lord, hear my prayer.

Living Word

God, I want to hear from You.

Ecclesiastes 3:1–8

For everything there is a season, and a time for every matter under heaven:

a time to be born, and a time to die;
a time to plant, and a time to pluck up what is planted;
a time to kill, and a time to heal;
a time to break down, and a time to build up;
a time to weep, and a time to laugh;
a time to mourn, and a time to dance;
a time to cast away stones, and a time to gather stones together;
a time to embrace, and a time to refrain from embracing;
a time to seek, and a time to lose;
a time to keep, and a time to cast away;
a time to tear, and a time to sew;
a time to keep silence, and a time to speak;
a time to love, and a time to hate;
a time for war, and a time for peace.

index

acknowledgments

I am forever indebted to those who have been a kind sounding board for my feelings.

I want to say a special thanks to Mindy for teaching me that sensitivity is a strength and Kara for showing me how to be courageous even when it isn't convenient.

Thank you, Mom, for welcoming my full range of emotions and my sisters for holding my feelings my entire life.

Thank you, Dad, for believing in my dream.

Thank you, Ashley, Kristin, Krissa, January, Katie, Erin, Becca, Aly, Greta, Jessica, KJ, Amanda, Gina, Jenn, Melissa, and Becky for your friendship.

Thank you to my church family.

Thank you to the beautiful souls at The Hope House. You are forever in my heart.

Thank you, Jackie Sevier, for your godly guidance.

A huge thanks to Jennifer Dukes Lee, my editor and friend, whose wisdom helped me breathe life into this book at the most critical moment.

Lisa Jackson, my agent, thank you for believing in this book from the very beginning and helping me get unstuck along the way.

Thank you to my kids, Manoah, Samuel, Noelle, Hannaly, and Mea. I love walking with you through every feeling you feel. It is the greatest honor of my life.

And, Sam, thank you for stopping that day by the lake to see me. That moment and every moment since, you have loved me. Your love is like water.

Anjuli Paschall grew up in San Diego. She studied psychology at Point Loma Nazarene University and earned her graduate degree from Talbot Seminary in spiritual formation and soul care. She has been married for close to twenty years to her childhood friend Sam. Together, they founded Sojourn and Sage, a retreat and residency home for the weary. They have five beautiful children: Manoah, Samuel, Noelle, Hannaly, and Mea. Anjuli is the author of *Stay* and *Awake*. As a pastor's wife, writer, and spiritual director, she learned that feelings are the pathway to prayer. She loves chai tea, golden hour, and the color orange.

CONNECT WITH ANJULI:

AnjuliPaschall.com

SojournAndSage.com

@lovealways.anjuli

@sojournandsage